RURAL ENGLAND

What's happening month by month

JILL MASON

PHOTOGRAPHS BY DAVID MASON

MERLIN UNWIN BOOKS

First published in Great Britain by Merlin Unwin Books Ltd, 2007

ISBN 978 1 873674 97 0

Published by:
Merlin Unwin Books Ltd
Palmers House
7 Corve Street, Ludlow
Shropshire SY8 1DB, U.K.

British Library Cataloguing-in-Publication Data:
A catalogue record for this book is available from the British Library.

Title page photo: the Sussex Weald.
Designed and typeset in Minion by Merlin Unwin Books Ltd.
Printed by Butler & Tanner Ltd, Frome, Somerset.

CONTENTS

INTRODUCTION

I have always lived in the countryside and it is as important to me as the air that I breathe. When I set out to write this book I was well aware that I knew a little about a lot of things but not an awful lot about anything in particular (except perhaps hares). One of the most intriguing things I found about England, is the short distance you need to travel to discover a totally different landscape and sometimes very noticeable local dialects. Of all the things I would miss most about England, I think the changing seasons would come top of the list. Maybe our weather isn't the most predictable but we still have our four distinct seasons. In fact every single month is different, from January when the first yellow aconites peep out of the ground, to December when a singing robin brightens a dreary day and red-berried holly decorates our homes.

In this surreal age of space travel, instant worldwide communications and high-tech mechanisation, it is easy to forget that what we see today has evolved over the last 8,000 years. From our more recent history, windmills and watermills stand in many parts of the English countryside as reminders of how our ancestors managed before engines were invented. The rich built magnificent mansions in acres of parkland as a visible sign of their wealth and after invading England in 1066 the Normans constructed great castles to protect their newly-acquired territories.

Anglo-Saxon peoples arrived from across the North Sea in the 5th century, helping to shape our language of today. Originally they were pagans from whom many of our customs and festivals have been inherited. In their simplistic way, they looked to nature for their beliefs, their hopes and their fears, but by the end of the 7th century they had converted to Christianity. Grass-covered hill-top forts, straight roads and Hadrian's Wall remain as legacies of the Roman invasion 2,000 years ago and preceding them Iron Age Man had discovered how to smelt iron. Bronze Age Man lived between 500 and 2,000BC and has left behind artefacts and evidence of his activities and settlements.

But before all that, after the last Ice Age, Neolithic Stone Age Man began it all 7,000 years ago by starting to clear the wildwood which then covered England. His descendents constructed the henges, standing stones and barrows, often marking burial sites, which stand symbolically today as constant reminders of our past.

Recycling is not a new concept, for our predecessors wasted nothing. Animals were killed for food and the skins used as clothing; horns or antlers were made into utensils or tools and the bones crushed to make fertilizer. Woodlands were cherished as they provided shelter, heat, implements, medicines and food. Man had to survive on whatever nature provided and cared for it accordingly. Our ancestors instinctively recognised that it was not in their interest to abuse or destroy.

Traditional rural skills are still with us, passed down through countless generations. Farm animals evolved over the centuries to suit different localities and many breeds were unique to particular areas. Most have now become extremely rare, none more so than the wild Chillingham cattle who are direct descendents of the cattle which once roamed over much of England.

While researching this book, I have delved deeply for facts and some of the most interesting came to light when I visited the Chillingham cattle (*see picture below*). They must surely be one of the rarest animals in the world, for only 66 now survive. Records show that they have been at Chillingham, Northumberland, for more than 700 years with no domesticated blood ever having been introduced. In 1947 numbers reached an all-time low of 13.

Many other species have died out through in-breeding and scientists are baffled as to why this hasn't happened to the Chillingham herd. But this extraordinary English breed has a strict,

self-imposed regime of killing any beast touched by humans; and all Chillingham baby calves have to be approved by the 'king' bull before being accepted within the herd, which has meant that no genetic weaknesses have ever been tolerated, thus ensuring the herd's survival.

During the past 40 years has come the realisation that the preservation of England's rare domesticated breeds and the immense diversity of wild flora and fauna in our fast-disappearing countryside, is of urgent national importance. Much work is now being undertaken by conservation bodies and after several bleak years the health of our countryside is noticeably improving.

Tractors may have replaced horses but the same cycle of ploughing, sowing, harvesting and tending livestock continues on farms throughout each year. The vibrancy of the countryside is obvious in spring, summer and autumn with plants flowering and seeding, insects busy, birds and animals multiplying. Hundreds of rural events take place providing a host of different leisure activities.

In winter, England may appear to be a drab place but a sharp frost or a fall of snow can instantly transform the landscape into a sparkling wonderland. The countryside moves at a much slower pace during these dark cold months. Certainly the insects and plants are mostly dormant but birds are plentiful if you know where to look. Little summer visitors from the south forsake us only to be replaced with large wildfowl winging their way from the frozen north. Bird-watching at any time of year can be rewarding. Spotting animals in winter is more challenging, for most tend to be nocturnal and some even hibernate. But even when the days are short, there is still plenty to see and do, although most activities have to be self-initiated. If you are equipped with warm waterproof clothing, rural activities can be all the more enjoyable without throngs of people – and the views are clearer with no leaves on the trees.

Rural England at any time of year is an amazing place. It is like a giant jigsaw made up of many parts. Look closer and you will find it crammed with history, local customs, agriculture, wildlife, plants, and geological features. If you are observant and have an enquiring mind, it is impossible to set foot in the countryside, whatever the season, without being confronted with myriad diverse and intriguing things. It is there to be seen, heard, smelled, sensed and felt; waiting to be investigated, experienced and appreciated.

The journey through each year is a rewarding one of discovery. The more we look, the more we find, as this book is intended to show.

Jill Morgan

August 2007

JANUARY

After a night when fog has combined with a sub-zero temperature, every tiny droplet of moisture becomes frozen, and this creates a hoar frost. Little ice crystals form rime on every twig, leaf and blade of grass which sparkle brightly against a clear blue sky if the sun breaks through. Sadly, this winter scene is rare and brief, for the very warmth of the sun soon destroys this stunning spectacle. Still, it doesn't always need snow to capture the magic of an English winter.

Wassailing on Twelfth Night

The ancient custom of wassailing originally asked for health for all crops and animals, but it is now principally associated with apple trees. Traditionally, it is celebrated on the old Twelfth Night, or the Sunday closest to it, and acquired its name from the Anglo-Saxon 'wes hal' meaning 'be in health'.

Many places, particularly in cider-making areas such as Devon and Somerset, still hold wassailing ceremonies. Traditional Morris dancers perform around the chosen apple tree. A toast of cider is drunk and what remains is either poured over the roots, or slices of toast are dipped in it and placed upon the branches by children. Supposedly this will bring good luck by attracting robins, although in folklore these birds are often associated with ill fortune. Finally, a shot is fired through the branches to ward off evil and awaken the good spirits in the orchard, and the tree from its winter slumber.

Although its popularity declined in the 1800s, Morris dancing has been keenly revived throughout England and the blackened faces of the dancers at the wassailing ceremony stem from the time when poor farm workers would dress up and dance to earn some extra money on a Sunday. When this was forbidden, they blacked their faces in the hope they wouldn't be recognised.

Morris or Molly dancers also symbolically re-enact another ancient custom, that of blessing the Plough. Plough Monday is still traditionally celebrated in many places on the second Monday in January, the night before ploughboys returned to work after Christmas. Dressed in colourful rag coats they collected money as they dragged a plough through the village before it was blessed in church.

The ancient custom of wassailing is re-enacted by Morris dancers around an apple tree at Ryton in Warwickshire.

Heathland Conservation Work

Conservationists use many tools, including flocks of sheep, to create the right habitat for the species they are trying to protect. Scrub clearance is often vital and rank grasses need to be kept at bay, which is where sheep, ponies and cattle can play such a valuable role.

Heaths were formed from the prehistoric clearance of native woodland but during the last century 90% of lowland heaths have been lost to forestry, farming, and neglect. Some are grassland while others are covered in heather and can still be seen at places like

Above: Winter grazing with sheep is used by conservationists as part of the management strategy to restore and maintain grassy heaths.

3

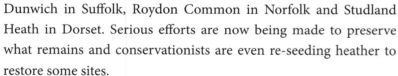

Dunwich in Suffolk, Roydon Common in Norfolk and Studland Heath in Dorset. Serious efforts are now being made to preserve what remains and conservationists are even re-seeding heather to restore some sites.

Several species of birds favour heathland habitat including the secretive Dartford Warbler (*Sylvia undata*) found in southern England and which may sometimes be spotted flitting around in gorse bushes.

The migratory stone curlew (*Burhinus oedicnemus*) was once common on ancient grassland in 23 counties of England but as their habitat disappeared, so did they. They are smaller than the common curlew and not related to it. In Spring 1985 only 160 pairs arrived in England to breed, so it was decided that protection was overdue.

Stone curlews choose to nest on bare ground. They used to

be able to find this on heaths, downlands and plains where sheep and rabbits kept vegetation grazed very short. But as heaths were ploughed up, sheep numbers declined and the huge number of rabbits was dramatically reduced when myxomatosis decimated the population in the early 1950s and the stone curlew were then forced to find nesting sites on arable fields. Farm machinery got bigger and faster and many nests were inadvertently destroyed.

Conservation measures now include searching arable fields in areas where pairs of stone curlew have been sighted so that their nests can be marked and avoided by the tractor drivers.

Above left: The secretive Dartford warbler is resident all year and inhabits the coastal heaths of southern England.
Above right: The rare stone curlew is a beneficiary of conservation work on grassland heaths which it visits in the summer.

Active management of the remaining ancient grasslands is also practised. On Salisbury Plain, amid military training activities, some sites have been cleared to encourage the stone curlew to nest. Attempts are also being made there to re-introduce the bustard, a large turkey-sized bird, which once shared the same habitat as the stone curlew but which became extinct in the mid-1800s.

Overall, the conservation efforts for stone curlew are proving successful, its range is spreading and numbers are rising. In 2005, 250 pairs migrated from their wintering grounds in Morocco, southern Spain and southern Portugal to breed in the drier parts of Wiltshire, Hampshire and on the Breckland heaths of East Anglia where they are also known as 'Thick knee' or 'Norfolk plover'.

Below: Red deer on the grassy heaths around Thetford, Norfolk.

Outdoor Leisure in January

Some riders enjoy the thrill of competitive mounted sports while others take pleasure from a ride in the countryside

Until the end of the Second World War the majority of horses and ponies in England were kept for work, but as people have become more affluent, so riding for pleasure has become increasingly popular. Young, old and disabled alike can enjoy the experience.

More than two and a half million people in the UK ride and it is a leisure activity that takes many forms. The countryside is criss-crossed with bridleways to ride, which in some places have been linked to form long-distance trails with accommodation for both horse and rider along the way. In holiday areas such as Exmoor, pony trekking is a popular way to discover the local countryside. With the

financial need to diversify, some farmers have opened up marked trails across their land suitable for riders of all ages and abilities. Several miles in length, these trails include the option of fences and other obstacles to negotiate which can make the ride more interesting and testing.

Riders seeking more of a challenge can satisfy their desire for speed and danger by competing in Point-to-Points. These are held between January and June and provide an introduction for both young horses and amateur riders to steeplechasing under the rules of National Hunt Racing. The Point-to-Point course includes ob-

Runners at the West Norfolk Hunt Point-to-Point at Fakenham. Many steeplechase horses and jockeys learn their trade at Point-to-Points.

stacles such as hedges, fences and ditches. A horse has to qualify to run in a race by having been taken out hunting on several occasions during the season. Although hunting hares and foxes with dogs was banned in England in February 2005, hunts have adapted to hunting within the law and horses which have attended these new hunt activities are eligible. Point-to-Points are organised at a local level by Hunts or a Point-to-Point Club. Sometimes they are held at rec-ognised race courses but usually special courses are laid out across farmland, often shared by more than one hunt.

The name 'steeplechase' originates from the 18th century when bets were wagered as to which rider would be first to reach a distant church steeple, riding cross-country. Although national hunt rac-ing can take place throughout the year it is predominantly a winter sport, replaced by flat racing between spring and autumn.

Acrid smoke billows upwards as a hot
shoe is tried against the horse's hoof.

The Work of
the Farrier

The practice of shoeing horses was brought
to England by the invading Romans who
put iron shoes on their horses' feet to protect them from lameness.

In the past, when donkeys and oxen
were used as draught animals they too
were shod. Each of the ox's cloven feet was
given two small half-moon-shaped iron
shoes: eight per ox.

A person who specialises in shoeing
horses, a farrier, is a highly skilled worker
who has served more than four years as an
apprentice. As well as the shoeing skills,
a thorough knowledge of the anatomy
of the horse is also taught because some
physical problems can be corrected with
specially-designed shoes.

Successful apprentices are awarded
a Diploma of the Worshipful Company
of Farriers (DipWCF), but the highest
qualification in farriery is the Fellowship
of the Worshipful Company of Farriers
(FWCF).

Horses' hooves, like our fingernails,
keep growing, and there is no feeling in
the outer edges. Hooves are fairly soft
and, if shoes are not put on, can easily become damaged. If a horse is not ridden or
worked then it is not necessary to have it
shod, although its feet will still need regu-

lar attention. While the shoe is heated in a forge the farrier trims the outer hoof as well as the horny triangular centre part, known as the 'frog', which acts as a shock absorber.

The shoe is hammered into shape on an anvil and tried for size, the hot metal leaving an outline on the newly pared hoof. Any necessary adjustments can then be made. Finally the shoe is quenched in a water trough before being fixed in place with nails hammered into the shoe and at an angle through the lower wall of the hoof.

The sharp protruding ends of the nails are then cut off. The procedure is painless and most horses quietly accept being shod. In normal use, shoes need replacing about every six weeks. Today, there are mobile farriers who bring their equipment in the back of a van, and shoes which are ready-made, so only minor adjustments are needed and they may even be put on cold. Plastic shoes are occasionally used and race horses are shod with lightweight aluminium shoes for racing. Studs can be fitted into the shoes if the surface is slippery.

The game of 'quoits' dates back to the 14th century and originated from competitions to see how many horse shoes could be thrown over a peg stuck in the ground.

Above: A pile of worn, discarded horseshoes begin to rust.

A horseshoe glows red in the hot coals of a farrier's furnace

Grey and Red Squirrels

Here is a mammal which does not hibernate during the winter, and which can be spotted in the leafless trees in January. The very attractive red squirrel (*Sciurus vulgaris*), with its winter-time ear tufts and thick bushy tail, is a native of England and until the 1950s was widespread in pine forests across the countryside.

Although described as red, there can be quite a variation between a deep rich chestnut and light sandy colour. Sadly, apart from the far north of England, only a few isolated colonies remain in places such as the Isle of Wight, Brownsea Island (off the Dorset coast) and around Formby in Lancashire where they have become very tame. Their demise was brought about by the introduction of the grey squirrel (*Sciurus carolinensis*) from North America in the 1870s.

Almost twice the size of the red, the grey squirrel has gradually elbowed its way across the country, bringing with it squirrel pox, a virus causing severe skin lesions, to which greys themselves are immune but to which reds are extremely vulnerable. Conservationists are doing their best to protect reds in areas where they still survive. Apart from the threat from greys, road traffic accounts for many casualties. On busy roads, warning signs are sometimes erected and ropes suspended overhead between the tops of trees so that the little red squirrels are able to cross safely.

Both species make nests high up in trees for shelter and in which to raise their young. These 'dreys' are constructed from twigs, strips of bark and leaves, and are lined with grass. Although not so active during the winter, neither species hibernate, but periods of very cold weather may cause them to lie up for several days.

In autumn, squirrels store food for winter by burying it in the ground. In their natural habitat reds feed primarily on the seeds found in pine cones but greys are not so fussy about their diet and those living in suburban parks often become very tame if food is put out for them. Where the two species exist in the same area, the

An invader from North America, the grey squirrel is not always a welcome guest.

smaller reds usually lose out in the competition for food. Endearing as they look, greys can be destructive animals, demolishing bird feeders with their sharp teeth and causing damage to trees by stripping the bark. Their teeth grow constantly, so gnawing on wood keeps them short.

Grey Squirrels are also not averse to taking eggs and young chicks from nests and can have a marked effect on the survival of songbirds. The name 'squirrel' is said to have originated from a Greek word meaning 'shade tail'.

Red (*see below*) and grey squirrels may remain in their dreys for several days during very cold weather, but do not hibernate.

Food and Shelter in the Winter

Ivy (*Hedera helix*) is common everywhere and unhindered will quickly envelop trees, walls and buildings. It is a vigorous perennial climber and although often described as a parasite it actually develops roots in the ground, from which it draws nourishment. A trunk of ivy can measure up to 10 inches (25cms) in diameter. However, hair-like aerial roots also grow from the trailing and climbing branches which enable the plant to cling tenaciously to tree trunks and penetrate walls.

Considerable damage can be caused to walls if the mortar is in poor condition. Ivy produces an abundance of small evergreen leaves and in September and October greenish flowers are borne in a many-flowered umbel on the tips of some of the shoots. Later, dark coloured berries develop in clusters.

Because of its autumnal flowering, ivy provides a valuable late feed for bees; and the berries are much sought-after by woodpigeons and other birds throughout the winter. It also provides a dry sheltered place where moths, butterflies and snails can hibernate in the winter. In Spring, many species of bird choose to nest in it.

Deer will browse on the leaves where ivy grows in woodland.

widespread and can be found growing in many places including sandy grassland and heaths.

It is also known as 'furze' or 'whin' and it is possible to find it flowering in most months of the year although less so in mid-summer when small, seed-bearing pods develop.

There are two other, less common species of gorse. Dwarf gorse can be discovered on acid soils in the south and east of England, such as the Dorset heaths and Dunwich Heath in Suffolk. Western gorse occurs mainly in the west and is often seen on coastal heathland.

An old country saying has it that when the gorse ceases to bloom then the kissing stops. As Dwarf and Western gorse come into flower between July and September, when Common gorse is not showing much colour, the kissing is guaranteed to continue throughout the year.

The height to which it has been eaten (the browsing line) will indicate which species of deer are present. A small muntjac cannot reach as high as roe, and a roe cannot reach as high as a red deer.

In winter the vibrant yellow flowers of Common gorse (*Ulex europaeus*) often add a bright splash of colour to an otherwise dreary landscape. It is a small dense evergreen shrub which bears yellow flowers on its numerous short green branches tipped with very sharp spines. A member of the pea family, Common gorse is

Opposite: All deer browse ivy leaves but a particularly low browsing line indicates that the small muntjac is present.
Above: Frost etches every individual ivy leaf.
Right: Common gorse, in flower most of the year, especially winter.

Wildfowl's Winter Refuge

Huge numbers of migratory swans and wildfowl rely in winter on conservation areas managed by the Wildfowl and Wetlands Trust, such as Martin Mere in Lancashire, Welney in Norfolk and Slimbridge in Gloucestershire. These reserves become busy places when the wildfowl start to arrive in October.

Unlike some of the other reserves, Welney does not have a resident captive collection. It is sited in the Ouse washes, about 20 miles long by a mile wide, which extend between the Old Bedford and Hundred Foot rivers. These washes are flooded in winter, acting as a safety valve for the surrounding low-lying Fens. In a complex system, sluice gates are opened and the washes take up the floodwater until the threat recedes; then the water is allowed to return to the rivers.

At Welney, familiar Mute swans are joined in autumn by Whooper swans (*Cygnus cygnus*) which fly in from their breeding grounds in Iceland. Travelling about 300ft (100m) above the sea or ground, they average 60mph but have been recorded at a height of over 26,000ft (8,200m) and at speeds of 100mph.

Guided across the Atlantic Ocean by the stars at night, they leave Iceland in early October when the weather conditions and wind direction are right. Thirteen hours later they reach the west coast of Scotland where they break their 1,200 mile (1,900km) journey for a brief rest before continuing south to Welney, making use of landmarks to find their way during daylight. Whoopers, with their distinctive yellow bills, are sometimes found in the company of visiting Bewick's swans which are very similar in appearance but slightly smaller and which fly in from the opposite direction, having migrated 2,200 miles (3,500 km) from Arctic Russia.

Every winter thosands of Whooper swans migrate from the far north to wetland areas of England such as Welney, Norfolk.

Greylag geese and many species of wild duck, including shoveler, tufted duck, teal and pochard (*Aythya ferina*), also arrive in large numbers. They are joined by wigeon which migrate from the northern regions of Lapland, Russia and Iceland. Unlike other duck species which feed predominately on aquatic plants and creatures, wigeon forage on land; neither do they quack but instead make a whistling sound.

A scramble of Pochard at Welney, Norfolk.

Viewing hides make it possible to observe most of these birds. Although swans and wildfowl find food on the surrounding marshes and farmland, this is supplemented with grain, and at feeding times after dark it is a spectacular sight to see the floodlit melee of ducks and swans jostling for a share of the barley put out for them.

15

Feeding Livestock in the Lean Months

There is little grass for farm livestock to eat during the winter months. Many native breeds could survive the winter outside but continental breeds are not so hardy. Either way, most cattle are brought into yards from November until April. Silage, made during the summer, constitutes a staple part of their diet.

Grass doesn't grow much in winter and when the weather is very wet the feet of heavy cattle sink into the ground, turning fields into a quagmire, so it is best to keep them indoors. Sheep don't damage the ground so much and with their insulating layer of greasy wool they are better equipped than cows to withstand the cold and wet weather. They too may need supplementary feeding, particularly those which are kept in mountain and moorland districts. Lowland sheep are more likely to find better quality grazing and it is common practice to move hill sheep from upland farms to lower ground for the winter where possible.

Before 2006 sheep and cattle farmers received a subsidy for each head of livestock but these payments are being phased out to be replaced with environmental grants paid for each hectare of land that is farmed. Stocking rates are being lowered for hill farmers and this could ultimately affect the habitat on hills and moorland.

In the long term this may result in noticeable changes, for the constant nibbling of sheep helps keep back invasive plants such as bracken and scrub.

The presence of livestock supports insect and invertebrate life; their droppings add goodness to the land and if a beast should die, and the carcase isn't found by the farmer, it provides food for insects, birds and wild animals. Much of the unspoiled beauty of English uplands is the result of knowledgeable management by countless generations of hill farmers.

Above: Mangel-wurzels were once tradition-ally grown for winter feed but these cows on a Nottinghamshire farm now have to make do with fodder beet.

Left: Most cattle are kept in yards during the winter and silage, made in the summer from grass, provides the bulk of their diet.

Right: Sheep kept out on the Fells of Cumbria are also grateful for a bite of silage in the middle of winter.

English Carrots All-year Round

Carrot seed sown in early January is covered with polythene to speed up germination and growth.

In areas of light, free-draining land, even as early as January if conditions are right, a start is made in sowing carrots. When the soil is dry enough, it is cultivated and ridged before large machines sieve out any stones, burying them inbetween the ridges. The carrot seed is then sown directly into the resulting fine tilth. Rolls of polythene are laid out on top of the rows to protect the carrots and to enhance the warmth of the soil. The polythene sheets are perforated so that water can seep through when it rains and because it is clear, the seeds quickly germinate. As the plants develop, the lightweight sheet is pushed up and does not restrict their growth. It is finally removed when the weather is warmer at the end of April or beginning of May.

By creating a greenhouse environment for their carrots, farmers can produce an earlier crop than could be obtained under natural conditions in England's unpredictable climate. Some of the earliest crops are gathered by hand and sold in bunches with the green tops still on. The majority of carrots though are harvested with giant machines which cut off the tops as they are lifted. They are then taken to packing stations where they are washed, sorted and packed. Carrot sowing continues from January until mid-summer and mature carrots are covered later in the year with straw to protect them from frost during the winter months. With this careful management, a year-round supply of home-grown English carrots is available in our shops.

FEBRUARY

The village of Cley-next-the-Sea is a typical north Norfolk village, the narrow road twisting through it flanked with quaint flint cottages. Until the 17th century, Cley was one of East Anglia's principal ports exporting grain and wool, but in 1637 a local landowner attempted to reclaim land which resulted in the river Glaven gradually silting up.

Today a vast area of reed beds and marshland separate the village from the sea which is only held at bay by a shingle bank. For centuries the sea and nearby marshes, together with local farms, ensured the inhabitants were self-sufficient, but now Cley relies almost entirely on tourism. The Cley windmill (*above*), built in the early 18th century, ceased to function in 1919 and fell into disrepair. It was converted into a holiday home in 1921 and is now run as a guest house with self-catering accommodation in the out-buildings. Occasionally, coastal reed beds are subject to flooding when high tides and strong on-shore winds conspire together to breach the defences, as happened around Norfolk in 1953 with the loss of many lives, and to a lesser extent more recently in 1996.

England's Oldest Winter Fair

Lynn Mart is the first fair in the showmen's calendar. It is the oldest in the country, having taken place since 1204 when King John granted the town its first charter. In 1537 Henry VIII granted another charter for two weekly markets, one in February on the Tuesday Market Place and the second in August on the Saturday Market Place. Also at that time the name of the historic medieval

Lynn Mart opens on Valentine's Day each year, ever since King John granted its first charter in 1204.

port was changed from Bishop's Lynn to King's Lynn. In 1559 a renewal charter ensured that the February mart became an annual event. Originally it would have been only for trading but gradually it has been replaced with a funfair.

Frederick Savage was a local engineer who built new rides. He pioneered the use of steam power for fairground barrel organs and went on to develop an industry producing steam-powered roundabouts and swings. In the 1870s he founded St Nicholas' ironworks to construct his new rides and Lynn Mart provided the perfect show case for his new inventions. Perhaps his most ornate were the 'gallopers'. In 1897 Lynn Mart became the place where Randall Williams introduced the public to moving pictures for the first time.

Traditionally Lynn Mart opens on Valentine's Day, February 14th, and showmen gather there from across the country. It is still held on the Tuesday Market Place which covers about three acres and is one of the largest in England.

At midday a bell is rung to announce the arrival of a procession of the town's mayor, accompanied by local dignitaries. They crowd together on the platform shared with bumper cars and the opening ceremony commences. Prayers are said for a successful mart and the original proclamation is read.

Thanks are given by an official of the Showmen's Guild of Great Britain and then it is time for everyone to try out the attractions. Local people can enjoy all the thrills and fun of the fair for the next two weeks although often the weather can at best be described as inclement.

Left: The original proclamation granting the Fair is read.
Above: A local Mayor and Mayoress enjoy the Fair with an 800-year history.

21

The Icy Grip of Winter

In the depths of winter there is little plant growth. Corn that was sown in the autumn and had grown a few inches remains static and will not be triggered into growth again until warmer weather arrives. The ground will sometimes be frozen hard and work on the land is brought to a halt. This was once a predictable occurrence during January or February but latterly English winters have become less harsh and snowfall has been sparse.

The cold also stops the growth of grass, so livestock need supplementary feeding. In the lowland cereal-growing areas of England, many acres of land will have been sown with turnips after the corn was cut in August. Sheep can then be fed on these throughout the winter, first eating off the green tops before gnawing on the roots.

Wattle or chestnut hurdles were once used to enclose them but now electric fences confine them to one part of the field at a time. When they have cleared that, the fence is moved, allowing them access to fresh ground. The term for this is to 'fold' sheep across the crop.

Many sheep from marsh and hill areas are transported to spend the winter feeding on fields of turnips or the left-overs from the sugar beet harvest, for they also find the tops and sweet chips left lying on the ground very palatable.

Payment for this 'winter keep' is usually made at a weekly rate per sheep; and arable areas, which are mostly devoid of sheep all through the summer, seasonally play host to many thousands of them. Not only do they provide useful additional income but their droppings also add goodness to the soil.

Upland farmers benefit through being able to take some of their sheep off the hills and moors. With little good quality grassland on their farms it is difficult for them to make sufficient hay or silage and winter weather conditions can make the high ground a hazardous place to keep livestock. By sending them away, young sheep will fatten faster than they would on the poor grazing, and pregnant ewes return home in Spring in good condition.

Left: Cold weather halts the growth of winter wheat.
Above: Turnips sown after the last harvest, make nourishing winter fodder for sheep.

The International Face of the English Countryside

As the need for farmers to diversify has become more urgent, the search for ways of increasing income has broadened. An unlikely answer has been to invest in alpacas (*Vicugna pacos*) for wool production. For the last twenty years, numbers have been built up through breeding from stock originally imported from Chile, Peru and Bolivia in South America where they are indigenous.

Alpacas have been domesticated for more than 5,000 years and were originally kept high in the Andes by the Incas. There are now approximately 15,000 alpacas in the UK. Their high quality wool is exceptionally fine and lustrous, and top grades command high prices. There are two types, the Suri which has a dreadlock type fleece and the Huacaya which possesses a fluffy coat and is the breed most commonly kept in the UK.

The fleece is clipped once a year in Spring or early summer and yields about 8lbs (3.5 kgs). Alpaca wool comes naturally in 22 different shades and the fibres are very durable; only silk is stronger. Alpacas stand approximately 39 inches (100 cms) high at the shoulders and weigh up to 2 cwts (100 kgs). Pregnancy lasts for 11 months and the young, known as 'cria', are usually born in the Spring.

Alpacas have a strong herding instinct and are very protective. This instinct is utilized by some sheep farmers who run one or two alpacas with their ewes to protect young lambs from being attacked by foxes.

Above: English farmers have been forced to diversify: today alpacas graze on the South Downs in Sussex.

A Warm Job on the Coldest of Days

A blacksmith works with iron heated in a furnace until it glows orange and becomes pliable enough to bend. It can then be held in a pair of tongs and shaped with a hammer using an anvil as a base.

The blacksmith's workplace, the forge, or the 'smithy', was a feature in nearly every village until the 1950s. Coke was used to produce the fierce temperatures required for the furnace which could be intensified with the help of bellows. The dim light within a forge enables the blacksmith to guage the changing colour of the hot iron as it is tempered and forged.

The village blacksmith's work once involved making most of the tools used in the local fields, woods and gardens as well as repairing items such as farm implements. He would shoe horses as well, but strictly speaking this specialist is a 'farrier' who, in modern times, has to be highly qualified.

Today the work for a modern blacksmith, besides repairing farm equipment, is often that of making ornamental wrought iron items such as gates and fences which are still in big demand. Highly skilled blacksmiths are often busy with restoration work. Gas is now used as a convenient alternative to old-fashioned coke for heating

Below: A blacksmith surrounded by the tools of his trade. Nearly every English village had a forge until the 1950s.

the furnace as it is quick, clean, convenient and reliable.

The British Artist Blacksmith Association (BABA) was formed in 1978 to bring together blacksmiths from across the country with similar artistic interests. Many of these work with steel, bronze and copper in addition to iron and have become sculptors in their own right. BABA organises events such as 'forge-in' demonstration projects and master classes which provide an opportunity for hands-on experience.

Right: The anvil is used to hammer and shape hot iron straight from the furnace.

Below: The gates at Gressenhall Rural Life Museum were made by members of the British Artist-Blacksmith's Association in 1992.

Digging Deeper in February

Moles (*Talpa europaea*) are a common pest and have inhabited Britain for at least 7,000 years, although there are none in Ireland.

Moles are solitary animals, very antisocial and territorial, spending most of their lives underground. A male will tentatively seek out a mate in Spring and after a gestation period of about four weeks she will give birth to three or four young. These are born pink and helpless in a nest of leaves within a complex of chambers beneath an extra-large molehill known as a fortress. They are suckled for about a month and are actively encouraged to leave home when they are about ten weeks old.

It is these youngsters that are most likely to be seen above ground, where they are vulnerable to predation. Although cats and dogs often catch them, it is very seldom that they eat moles because their scent glands taint the flesh.

A mole's diet consists principally of earth worms, and lengthy tunnels connected to chambers are dug in their search for food. Moles need to eat more than half their bodyweight each day and construct pitfall traps to catch their prey. They have periods of frantic activity followed by time spent grooming and resting.

Moles have large powerful shoulders, a very short tail and dense velvety black fur. Occasionally white or cinnamon-coloured ones are discovered which seem to be local to certain areas. Possess-ing no visible ears and only rudimentary eyes, moles are equipped with a very sensitive pink nose and an acute sense of smell.

In one day they can travel up to three miles underground or dig 100 yards (90m) of new tunnel, periodically pushing this earth to the surface, creating 'mole hills' which ruin a well-kept lawn and cause damage to crops and machinery. They can excavate several pounds of soil in less than half an hour and create as many as eight molehills in 24 hours. Moles do not hibernate but in winter stay deeper underground. With warmer weather activity increases, usually in late March, and tunnels may be so close to the surface that the direction they take is obvious. In newly-sown crops, seedlings are pushed out of the ground and on grassland the grazing area may be much reduced.

There are now an estimated 31 million in Britain. There are many country names for the mole, most of them variations of 'Mouldiwarp'. Another descriptive expression is 'the little gentleman in black velvet' which is said to date back to 1702 when opponents of William III celebrated his death when he fell from his horse as it stumbled over a mole hill.

Above left: The common mole, enemy to the gardener, who often deters them with various devices including moth balls, bottles on sticks or little windmills stuck into the ground.

Above right: Pale or cinnamon-coloured moles are sometimes found in certain localities.

Silent Hunters

Thankfully the once-threatened English population of barn owls (*Tyto alba*) is now recovering and once again the silent ghost-like spectre is becoming a common sight in the countryside. In the 1960s the use of DDT badly affected the population of barn owls, along with many other birds of prey, resulting in their eggs failing to hatch because the shells had become thin. In addition, changes in farming policies meant: fewer meadows in which to find food; the conversion of barns into homes; and the removal of many hollow trees reduced resting and nesting sites.

Recent agricultural schemes such as set-aside and conservation headlands have improved habitat for the small mammals on which barn owls feed and nest boxes have proved very successful. Increasing traffic still poses a serious threat though as road verges provide an ideal hunting ground and inevitably there are casualties. As barn owls feed mainly on rodents they are highly valued as pest controllers and popular with everyone. However because they frequent churches and graveyards, and wheeze and screech like demons, they often instilled fear in our ancestors.

Although owls are generally considered to be nocturnal, the barn owl can often be seen systematically searching a field during daylight hours. When it spots something of interest it will hover above before dropping to the ground.

Above left: There are 205 species of owls worldwide but the barn owl is the most widespread, inhabiting every continent except Antarctica.
Above: Short-eared owls hunt over the moorlands of northern England.

Another owl active during the day is the little owl which is not a native to England but was introduced about a hundred years ago. This diminutive compact bird prefers farmland and hedgerows to woodland and inhabits holes in trees, buildings, straw stacks and sometimes even rabbit holes. When worried or puzzled it has the amusing habit of bobbing up and down. Its diet principally consists of invertebrates and insects.

Short-eared (*Asio flammeus*), long-eared (*Asio otus*) and tawny owls are three other species to be found in Britain. An owl's circular face is designed to focus light into the large rounded eyes and the slightest high frequency sound is directed to its ears enabling it to hunt by sound with incredible precision in the dark. Its feathers are soft and silent in flight but, because of its light bodyweight in proportion to its size, an owl finds it difficult to manoeuvre in strong winds.

Indigestible parts of its food such as bone and fur form into 'pellets' which are coughed up and can be found lying on the ground beneath an owl's perch. If these are dissected it is possible to identify what it has been feeding on. Incubation of the four or more eggs begins as soon as the first is laid so that they hatch in succession. It is then very much a matter of survival of the largest and fittest, should food be in short supply.

How many young eventually fledge is very dependant on weather conditions and availability of prey. In some years small rodents aren't very successful in breeding so there is a shortage of food for the owls to catch for their chicks.

Right: Long-eared owls are particularly well-camouflaged, making them difficult to spot in coniferous woods.

Signs of the End of Winter

The very welcome sight of snowdrops (*Galanthus nivalis*) in late winter indicates that the earth is once again stirring into life after the dereliction of winter. The plants, with their delicate white bell-shaped flowers etched with green, seem completely unfazed by even the severest of winter weather. Their resilience is incredible and some woodland gardens are opened up to the public in February for snowdrop walks, and churchyards are advertised, so that their beauty can be more fully appreciated.

Snowdrops are a common garden flower with several varieties being grown but they readily become established in the wild from discarded bulbs. They are not generally considered to be indigenous to Britain and were probably introduced from central Europe in medieval times.

Great swathes of white flowers beneath the bare trees in February indicate just how successful snowdrops have been in naturalising woodland. Traditionally they are said to appear around Candlemas (2nd Feb). In the Christian Church's calendar this is the Feast of the Purification of the Virgin Mary to whom snowdrops were dedicated, and on that day would be placed around her image. Like so many religious celebrations in England, Candlemas may well have been adapted from the pre-Christian Celtic 'Feast of Lights' which took place on the first two days of February, the mid-point between the shortest day and the spring solstice.

Catkins, or 'lamb's-tails' as they are affectionately known in the countryside, are the male flowers of hazel (*Corylus avellana*) one of the most useful shrubs to be found growing in woods and hedgerows. Immature flowers can be seen hanging on branches once the leaves have fallen in autumn and the slightest hint of warmth triggers them to develop.

Bottom left: All it needs is a little warm sunshine to trigger the growth of catkins.
Bottom right: 2nd February (Candlemas) is when the first snowdrops are traditionally said to appear.

Gentle breezes distribute clouds of the yellow pollen and, like snowdrops, catkins are a sure indication that Spring is on its way even in the apparent depths of winter.

Hazel branches are much sought-after by gardeners as the bushy ones are ideal for pea sticks, while the straighter ones make excellent stakes and supports for runner beans, and they can also be used as walking sticks. In late summer the tiny crimson female hazel flowers will have developed into delicious nuts which, unfortunately for us, impatient grey squirrels find very palatable and feast on before they have had time to properly ripen.

Above: Snowdrops, among the first of the bulbs to flower in Spring, flourish in moist, shaded soil.

31

Winter Reed-Cutting to Preserve a Unique Eco-System

The common reed (*Phragmites australis*) dominates marshy ground and forms dense areas. It is an unusual plant in that it can thrive in either salt or freshwater. It is the tallest of Britain's native grasses, growing over 6 feet (2m) in height around the water's edge and preferring to have its roots in water for most of the year.

For centuries reed has been cut and used for thatching buildings and for basket weaving. As local demand dwindled and wet areas were drained, it was realised that management through maintaining

water levels and regular cutting on a one or two year cycle was necessary to preserve this unique eco-system which supports the diversity of wildlife that can be found only in reed-beds.

One uncommon species reliant on this particular habitat is the bearded tit (*Panurus biarmicus*), often called bearded reedlings, or 'pingers' by bird watchers because of the sound of their flight calls. Confined to the south and east of England the bearded tit is actually Europe's sole member of the babbler family which frequents Africa and Asia.

The reed bunting (*Emberiza schoeniclus*) is another bird that inhabits reed-beds and the summer-visiting reed warbler also seeks out reeds in which to nest.

In late summer, swallows will sometimes assemble in reed-beds prior to their departure and in winter they are a favourite roosting place for starlings (*Sturnus vulgaris*). Although starling numbers are believed to have decreased by 50% during the last 40 years there is still an estimated population of 8.5 million and they show signs of making a come-back. Many species of insects, moths, beetles and snails are also dependent on reed habitats.

In recent years the value of reed-beds for water purification has been recognised and they are often now incorporated into eco-friendly developments as an effective and natural method for the treatment of waste water. This is purified as the growing reeds trap sediment and utilise nutrients in the water.

Opposite top: The rarely-seen bearded tit is also known as the bearded reedling.
Opposite left: Reed cutters at Cley-next-the-Sea, Norfolk.
Right: The reed bunting favours reed and sedge beds, but can be seen in fields and even gardens in harsh winters.
Below: In winter, huge flocks of starlings gather to roost, particularly in reed beds.

Clay Pigeon Shooting

An estimated one million people take part in shooting sports in England and 'clay pigeon shooting' is widely enjoyed by those who have no wish to shoot at living creatures or who wish to hone their shooting skills when live quarry is out of season.

'Trap' shooting began in the 18th century when live pigeons were released from under old hats (traps). Targets were also made of glass balls filled with feathers.

Then, in 1880, George Ligowsky from Cincinnati, USA, patented his invention of a terracotta disc-shaped 'clay pigeon' followed, two years later, by his design for a mechanical 'trap' to launch it in.

Needless-to-say his invention soon reached England. In 1921 it became illegal to release live birds from cages for trap shooting and the first clay pigeon shooting competition was held.

Since then, shooting at clays with a shotgun has grown in popularity and become an Olympic sport in which the English, men and women, excel. Modern clay targets are made from a mixture of limestone and coal tar pitch, and they come in several different colours and three different sizes. Standard has a diameter of 110mm, midi at 90mm and mini at 60mm.

There are clay shooting grounds all around the country. Competitions, with many variations in the way targets are presented, are held throughout the year.

There are moves to call the sport 'clay shooting' in preference to 'clay pigeon shooting' in order to erase any impression that live pigeons are being used. Many clay shoots are organised as fundraising charity events.

Above: Clay pigeon shooting in Essex. This is an increasingly popular sport, practised throughout the year.

MARCH

About one third of Exmoor (*above*) is in Devon, with the remainder in Somerset. The area was designated a National Park in 1954 and is the smallest in England, yet within its boundaries is a huge diversity of habitats and wildlife. Steep cliffs guard parts of the 34-mile (55 kms) coastline, making it inaccessible in many places. Here oak woodland is inhabited by a tribe of feral goats in the Valley of Rocks and around Lynton and Lynmouth. Sheep and small indigenous ponies have roamed free on the high moorland plateau for thousands of years, in the company of wild red deer. Deep wooded valleys known as 'combes' interlace the landscape offering the deer shelter when the weather is harsh. Farmers have long utilised the fertile soil of the vales. Some areas are covered with heather but most only support moor grasses and specialist plants which grow in numerous bogs. In 1869, R.D. Blackmore (1825-1900) chose Exmoor as the setting for his famous novel *Lorna Doone*.

A Taste of Rural England: Farmers Markets

Farmers Markets were originally set up in 1997, with the first held in Somerset. Since then they have grown in popularity and there are now over 500 in the UK, each one selling local produce. In 2002 a set of rules were introduced by the National Association of Farmers Markets, ensuring the products are all produced, caught or processed by the stallholder in person, within a defined local area.

Nearly half of all Farmers Markets are now registered with the FARMA scheme which provides assurance that these criteria are met. As farmers have sought ways in which to diversify and markets have developed, the tendency has been for many producers to create specialist products, which command higher prices, rather than selling off surplus farm produce.

The markets provide an outlet for a wide variety of goods including crafts, home baking, preserves, honey, vegetables, plants, cheeses, rare breed organic meat as well as fish, wild game and venison. It takes two years for a farm to become fully organic and ever-increasing demand outstrips production in England today. A new intermediary initiative promoting environmentally-friendly farming, but not necessarily organic, is known as LEAF (Linking Environment and Farming) and is helping to bridge that gap between supply and demand.

Farmers Markets are usually held at monthly intervals in towns and cities across England, sometimes more frequently. Among the benefits of these markets has been the interaction and greater understanding between country producers and urban dwellers. Farmers markets also have environmental advantages, with reduced packaging and transport costs and they have encouraged customers to

Left: The monthly Farmers' Market at Norfolk County Showground, near Norwich.

HANDS ON PRESERVES

AVAILABLE TODAY:

MADE IN NORFOLK

* GARLIC + HERB OIL
* SEVILLE ORANGE MARMALADE
* GRATED HORSERADISH
* GINGER, APPLE + WALNUT CHUTNEY
* PICKLED SHALLOTS
* CRANBERRY + DATE CHUTNEY
* PRUNES IN BRANDY

* APPLE + SULTANA CHUTNEY
* LEMON + LIME MARMALADE
* SPICY APRICOT + ORANGE CHUTNEY
* SPICED APPLE + RHUBARB CONSERVE
* BREAD + BUTTER PICKLE
* PICKLED RED CABBAGE
* RED ONION + CHILLI CHUTNEY

return to country town centres benefiting local shop keepers.

Rural producers are able to do away with the middleman, have a regular outlet for their products, come into contact with and possibly even educate, their customers.

Farmer's Markets are well worth a visit even if it is only to discover the diversity of items and skills that can be found in the locality and to discover how each item has been made, grown or obtained.

Above: An opportunity to sample and buy the home-made preserves on sale at the Farmer's Market at Creake Abbey in North Norfolk.

Seed Drilling and Muck Spreading

Drying winds in March enable farmers to resume cultivation of land that has been too wet all winter. As soon as soil conditions improve there is much haste to plant crops. Modern technology has made the job quicker, easier and more efficient. Drills accurately sow seeds at the correct density with rows an equal distance apart. The seed is often pre-dressed with chemicals to make it resistant to disease and pests. If you see the tractors out in March, Spring wheat, barley, rape and oats will be among the first seeds being sown, then possibly peas or grass seed.

It is also the time of year to sow root crops. Potatoes need to be planted in ridges and the seeds of sugar beet, which is grown extensively in the East of England, will need to be drilled. Sugar beet has only been grown in England since the early 1900s and was once a very labour-intensive crop. Horses were used to prepare the ground and sow the seeds and afterwards the crop would need thinning, known as 'singling' or 'chopping out', which was done by hand using a hoe. After that weed control was necessary, either by hand or with a horse-drawn hoe.

Modern technology has greatly speeded up the process of sugar beet production in England. Sprays and dressings control weeds and super-precision drills dispense the beet seeds singly at the required density, doing away with the need to thin the crop by hand.

The sowing of other more tender crops such as maize, linseed and salad crops will be done later in the Spring when the threat of

Above: Recycling muck is nothing new to farmers who have long appreciated the value of livestock manure for improving their crops.

hard frosts has diminished. Once seeds are in the ground they need sufficient warmth and moisture to make them germinate quickly and become well established.

During March, arable farmers are making the most of the improving ground conditions, and so too are livestock farmers who welcome the opportunity to get onto their grassland.

Farmyard manure is a valuable by-product of livestock housed inside during the winter and is the epitome of recycling. Solid waste excrement mixed with litter used for bedding is spread on fields in early Spring whenever the ground is dry enough to support the weight of a tractor without damage. Manure is a natural fertilizer which enriches grassland or, when spread on top and then ploughed in, provides nutrients and also organic material to improve the texture of the soil. Slurry (liquid manure without bedding litter) can be stored in a lagoon or large tank and is spread on the fields either by an irrigation system or tractor-drawn tanker.

Above: Seagulls follow the tractor as Spring barley is sown in March.

Ewes and Lambs

There are over forty different breeds of sheep native to Britain and recently many others have been imported from the Continent to improve fertility or build. A few of the best wool-producing native breeds are still kept pure by people specialising in spinning and weaving, but English wool production is now of little importance and cross-breeding is common practice for lamb production.

Breeds are often particular to a region; they have developed to best suit the habitat in which they live. Some have now become very rare while others remain as popular as ever.

Most of the breeds from high ground in the north of England have horns although not always both sexes. They are usually smaller, hardier and slower-maturing than the low-level sheep in order to survive the open hillsides and poorer grazing. Hill sheep are thus able to utilise ground that could not support any other crops or livestock.

Farmers with lowland sheep may aim to produce early-season lamb for consumption at Easter because this commands top prices.

Above: Swaledale sheep in the Yorkshire Dales.

Right: Cotswold sheep, known as 'Cotswold Lions' were famous for their high quality wool. They faced extinction before the Rare Breeds Survival Trust stepped in.

Sometimes these sheep will be kept indoors to have their lambs. Other farmers keep their sheep outdoors all the time, preferring to lamb them later when the weather is more benign and there is sufficient grass that they don't require supplementary feeding.

The majority of lambs are born in March and are welcomed as harbingers of Spring in the countryside. However, on the high ground, Spring arrives later and the hill sheep there are not generally lambed until well into April.

Ewes commonly have twins and sometimes even triplets, although they only have two teats. When they are born, all lambs have long tails but those kept on lush pastures are usually docked so that they don't get caked with excrement. Those destined to live out on the open hills and Fells are left with long tails to give them protection against the harsh weather.

Kept together with their mothers in a field, young lambs are a pretty sight as they form gangs and indulge in games of gambolling and racing.

Below: A flock of Exmoor Horn sheep with their lambs on the edge of Exmoor – no longer the common sight they once were.

The English Thatcher

A thatched cottage in a pretty country village is a quintessentially English image.

Roofs have been thatched with straw since 500BC. In more recent times straw and reed continued to prove useful in areas where slate was not available. Other local plant materials have also been used over the centuries, including heather, bracken, rushes and various grasses.

At present there are about 30,000 thatched buildings in Britain, of which 24,000 are 'listed' (giving protection from alteration or demolition) because they are of special historic or architectural interest. Generally, only water reed and wheat straw are now used.

The wheat straw has to be undamaged and is therefore not suitable if it has been through a combine harvester. As a result, thatching straw needs to be specially cut and cared for in the old-fashioned way. Before combine harvesters and mechanical balers came into general use in the late 1950s, corn was cut and tied into sheaves by a binder. These were subsequently loaded onto wagons and taken back to the farm where they were built into stacks.

Hay was always gathered loose and made into large stacks or 'ricks'. These had to be simply thatched to keep out the rain. So, until the combines and balers took over, there was work throughout the summer for thatchers if local farmers weren't able to thatch their own hayricks or straw stacks.

Straw can be thatched in two styles. One gives a slightly ragged appearance and the other is neatly trimmed. Water reed, more commonly known as 'Norfolk' reed, is superior to straw. Reed that has grown in that county is considered to be the best of all but a lot used for thatching in England today is imported from Eastern Europe or Turkey. Depending on the condition of the old thatch, the majority is usually removed to leave a thin layer on the rafters.

The fresh straw, or reed, is delivered in bundles which are carried up onto the roof and spread thickly over it. It is very carefully put in place, beginning at the bottom of the roof and working upwards, and fastened with metal binding hooks. Spars or 'broatches', which have been cut from split willow or hazel and then twisted, are still sometimes used to hold the thatch in place. The straw or reed is combed out with simple rakes, it is trimmed with long-handled knives or shears, then mallets and 'leggetts' are used to pat it into place.

The ridges of thatched houses are often capped with sedge. Small-mesh wire-netting safeguards the thatch which was once a favourite place for rats and house sparrows to make their home.

The largest density of thatched cottages can be found in the south-west of England and East Anglia. Although there are regional styles, much depends on the individual thatcher. Some add a finishing touch such as a thatch bird or cat on the ridge as their personal 'signature'.

Opposite: A broatch-maker in his workshop at Didlington, Norfolk. Broatches, used for securing the thatch, are made from split hazel or willow.

Above right: Thatching a cottage in Suffolk, using reed with sedge to complete the ridge.

The Mad March Hare

The Brown hare (*Lepus capensis europaeus*) is thought to have been introduced to England by the Romans and it is one of Britain's most fascinating creatures. Once common and widespread, the population is drastically reduced in some areas; although in certain regions of the country hares are still prolific. There are several reasons for the decline, but the principal causes are believed to be mechanisation of farming and loss of habitat. Many hares are killed by cars on the roads and by fast-moving farm machinery.

Although very similar in appearance to a rabbit, hares are almost twice the size and very different in their habits. They do not live in burrows. They can sometimes be found sheltering in woodland but in general they prefer the open countryside where they scrape out a 'form' in which to lie unobserved.

Hares prefer to remain out of sight, aided by their well-camouflaged coats, but all this changes in early Spring when caution is thrown aside.

The spectacle of hares 'boxing' in March is a moment never to be forgotten but it is not, as previously thought, two or more bucks fighting but a female trying to ward off the attentions of over-amorous males.

After a pregnancy lasting about six weeks, between two and six young are born, fully furred with their eyes open. No nest is made. They become active very quickly and within a day or so the doe will have split them up, leaving each hidden in different clumps of vegetation.

She returns to feed her babies only once a day, usually after dark, and they are weaned at about six weeks. From then on they have to fend for themselves. Needless to say they are very vulnerable to predation. The doe may produce three or even four litters a year but survival rates are poor. Their only defence is cunning, camouflage and speed. Adults can run at up to 45mph (72km).

A smaller species of hare, the indigenous Mountain hare, turns white in winter and lives on ground higher than about 1,500ft (460m). Although mainly confined to Scotland, there is a small population surviving in the Peak District.

Hares, with their erratic behaviour, have long been the subject of folklore, myth and superstition – often associated with ill-fortune, madness and witches. Even in this cynical age, these mysterious animals still capture the imagination.

Opposite above: Hares begin to act in an inexplicable manner in early March.

Opposite below: Young hares are called leverets and are born fully-developed.

Right: Mad March hares 'boxing' in a field of winter barley. Around this time of year, this normally reclusive, nocturnal animal often seems to throw all caution to the wind. The fighting usually occurs when a female rebuts the unwanted attentions of an unfavoured male.

Courting Woodcock and Snipe

The male Common Snipe (*Gallinago gallinago*), normally nocturnal and so well-camouflaged resting on the ground during the day, makes himself rather more obvious in Spring. To impress females, his courtship display involves rising into the sky and 'drumming' as he twists and descends. The whirring sound he makes is rather like a goat bleating – and is produced by vibrations of the outer tail feathers and not by the wing feathers as experts once thought.

Snipe are very much birds of the moorland, marsh and open bog. They were far more common in England before farmers drained the wettest fields, depriving them of their habitat. Recent conservation schemes to increase wetlands should help the numbers of these little birds to recover.

Snipe and woodcock (*Scolopax rusticola*) are classed as waders, but they are seldom found along the shoreline as most waders are. Although very similar in appearance they differ slightly in size and the easiest way to distinguish them is to note where they have been seen during daylight hours. They have a rapid zig-zag flight when disturbed. Their long bills are used to probe soft ground for insects, worms and other invertebrates.

The snipe's nest is hidden in a tussock of vegetation and around four eggs are laid which take nearly three weeks to hatch. The young leave the nest within a few hours and are able to fly a short distance by the time they are a fortnight old. The English population is boosted in early winter as other snipe leave the frozen bogs of Scandinavia and Russia to seek the milder English winter. Along with these migrants a few of their smaller cousins, the Jack snipe (*Lymnocryptes minimus*), arrive. These have a shorter beak and are fully protected by law.

Woodcock are birds of damp, mixed woodland, particularly favouring those with holly or rhododendrons. At night they seek out moist ground on which to feed, often alongside snipe. Wood-

Left: The woodcock's plumage blends well with dead leaves on the woodland floor.

cock are resident in England all year but their numbers are swelled in winter by migrants, particularly in the West Country.

At dusk in Spring the male woodcock will fly slowly over his territory uttering his distinctive call of three or four low-pitched croaks followed by a short high-frequency squeak. This ritual is known as 'roding'.

When danger threatens, the mother woodcock is said to move her chicks one at a time by flying away with them tucked between her thighs: although this theory is much disputed.

Above: The snipe's long beak is used to probe boggy ground for worms and other invertibrates.

Right: Jack snipe are less than 8 inches (20 cms) long from the tip of their beak to the tip of their tail.

Vernal Stirrings: Frogs and Toads

The Common frog (*Rana temporaria*) and Common toad (*Bufo bufo*) are amphibians and both are widespread in England. They emerge in early Spring when the urge to reproduce makes them seek out ponds or lakes in which to mate and lay their eggs.

This is a dangerous time, for often they need to cross roads to reach their traditional breeding places. Some underpasses have been built or voluntary wardens patrol strategic crossings on warm Spring evenings to help save their lives.

Frogs lay up to 2,000 eggs in clusters, each individually coated in a round globule of jelly. Toads spawn slightly later and their eggs, also encased in a jelly-like substance, are laid in a long double string up to 8ft (2.5m) in length. After two to three weeks their eggs hatch into tadpoles which live in the water and feed on algae and plants. As they grow in size, both pairs of limbs develop and gills are replaced with lungs. At this stage, in mid-summer, they leave the water and the tail is eventually absorbed. Few frog tadpoles reach maturity for at different stages they are at risk of falling prey to fish, newts, grass snakes, mammals and birds.

Toads and frogs are quite similar in appearance, but frogs have a smooth, moist skin whereas toads are slightly larger and their dry skin is covered with wart-like lumps. Toads mostly move about by crawling forwards on all four feet whereas frogs, which have longer hind legs, jump or hop.

Although amphibious, toads and frogs spend most of their lives

Above: Male frogs seek out the females in a shallow pond in early Spring. The eggs are fertilised by the male as they are released.

out of water, and toads especially can be found in surprisingly dry places, far from water. They both tend to be nocturnal and hibernate in winter, frogs choosing mud and toads a drier place.

The common frog is in decline due to pollution, loss of habitat and in some areas of England it has recently been affected by a deadly disease known as 'redleg'. Toads, because they taste unpleasant, are less likely to be predated: by far their greatest threat is the motor car. Toads have been known to live for as long as 50 years.

The Natterjack toad is a native species which is comparatively rare. Pool frogs, which died out in 1990 after colonising England during the last Ice Age, have been re-introduced into some small glacially-formed ponds known as 'pingoes' in Norfolk.

Folklore had it that frogs could cure whooping cough and lung infections and toads could spit poison which would make a pregnant woman go blind or miscarry. Toads have long been associated with the devil and witchcraft, perhaps because their skin contains poisonous substances and, unlike frogs, they are unpalatable to other creatures once they are fully grown.

Below: Toads are on the move in March, searching for ponds in which to lay their eggs.

Rare Breeds Back from the Brink

Many of our native breeds of horses and ponies were facing extinction by the end of the Second World War. Ponies provided meat during those times of hardship and probably worst affected was the Exmoor pony, whose numbers were reduced to just forty. Soon after the war, most of the remaining work horses and ponies were made redundant by mechanisation. Thankfully, the threat of extinction of all the English breeds was noticed just in time, and the future of our native ponies and horses now seems assured.

Before Victorian times, many different breeds of farm animal were distinct to various parts of England. Many of these have now become extremely rare, so the Rare Breeds Survival Trust, a national charity to conserve endangered breeds, was set up in 1971 by Mr Joe Henson who had already begun collecting them on his farm near Stow-on-the-Wold in the Cotswolds.

Over 70 breeds of cattle, sheep, pigs, horses, goats and poultry

Above: Ancient breeds such as the Exmoor pony nearly died out. Only about 250 still live semi-wild on the moor but their value has now been recognised and they are proving their worth by grazing and thus conserving habitats.

are listed by the RBST and are categorised as critical, endangered, vulnerable, at risk, or traditional. Some are even rarer than the Giant Panda. Obviously it takes longer to increase the stock of horses and cattle, which produce only one offspring each year, than it does for pigs or poultry which can multiply more quickly.

During the devastating outbreak of Foot and Mouth disease in 2001, which affected many parts of England, it became obvious that preserving the animals themselves might not be enough to safeguard the breeds, so the National Bank of Genetic Resources was established in which semen, embryos and other genetic samples could be stored. To be eligible, breeds must be native to the UK.

It is fun to travel across England spotting different local breeds. The northern uplands, for example, which are unsuitable for arable farming, are still very much home to traditional native sheep breeds such as Lake District Herdwicks and the very popular Swaledales. More than 25 breeds of sheep appear on the RBST register.

Ironically the recent upsurge in demand for naturally-grown or organic meat, for which people are prepared to pay high prices, may yet prove to be the saviour of the slower-growing English breeds of pigs, sheep and cattle.

Below: Large black pigs have gone out of fashion for commercial production because the public didn't like black rind on their bacon.

A Bankside View of England

For centuries water proved the most practical method of transporting goods around the country. Agricultural produce such as grain or wool could be taken to towns and cities and coal or other goods carried on the return journey. Large loads could easily be transported on barges pulled by horses.

Canals were first recognised as a practical way of linking rivers for transportation in the mid-17th century and virtually all goods manufactured during the industrial revolution were moved by water. In the early days canals were known as 'navigations' and were dug out by gangs of men using pick-axes and shovels who became known as 'navvies'. Canals have to be level and England isn't flat, so tunnels needed to be constructed through hillsides. Valleys and gorges had to be bridged by aqueducts. To negotiate lesser inclines 'locks' were devised to raise boats to different levels. With the arrival of railways and motor cars, our waterways went into a slow decline.

During the last 40 years some neglected canals have been restored and are now as busy ever but for a very different purpose. The original narrowboats were designed as barges for transporting goods and had only cramped living accommodation. These have been replaced by modern diesel-powered versions fully equipped for a comfortable holiday. There is now a 4,000-mile national network of navigable waterways but a trip aboard a narrow boat has to be taken at a very leisurely pace.

A holiday on the inland waterways offers a different perspective on rural England and is an excellent way of observing the countryside and its wildlife.

Above: Narrowboats at the top of Foxton Locks, Leicestershire – a flight of ten 'staircase' locks which will raise a boat 75 feet in 45 minutes.

APRIL

Widecombe-in-the-Moor (*above*) nestles amongst the blanket bogs, heather moorlands and ancient woodlands of Dartmoor in Devon. Hardy, semi-wild Dartmoor ponies roam the heathland and in Spring and summer, wild flowers attract thousands of insects and butterflies.

Time and man have sculpted the bleak landscape. Erosion over thousands of years has, in places, exposed the underlying granite to form rocky outcrops known as 'tors', the highest of which, High Willhays, is over 2,000ft (620m). Dartmoor was designated a National Park in 1951 and has the greatest density of Bronze Age remains anywhere in England.

Parts of the moor have been farmed since medieval times and small livestock farms still huddle in clusters within some of the more sheltered valleys. Other local industries have been the extraction of tin and kaolin. Dartmoor however is probably best known for the stark, grey prison set in its midst. Built in 1802 to house French prisoners from the Napoleonic Wars, two centuries later it still retains a notorious reputation.

Easter's Pagan Countryside Roots

Easter often falls in April. The date is not fixed but is set between March 22nd and April 25th. It is celebrated on the first Sunday after the first full moon following the vernal equinox, but can be adjusted so as not to coincide with the Passover festival. The timing of Easter has been disputed ever since it was first set by the Roman Emperor Constantine I, in 325AD. Many attempts have been made to fix the date: in fact in 1928 the British Parliament enacted a measure to commemorate Easter on the first Sunday after the second Saturday in April but it has never been adopted.

The ancient Saxons worshipped Eostra whose earthly symbol was the hare. They celebrated the return of Spring with the festival Eastre, later adopted by Christians as Easter. The association of eggs with the Spring ceremony also pre-dates Christianity: eggs were the symbol of fertility and rebirth and these Saxon beliefs have lingered to this day in the form of Easter egg hunts.

Many visitor attractions open at Easter and, after the cold dark days of winter, families find it a pleasure to discover once again that the countryside is waking from its winter slumber. However, commercialism on a grand scale has obscured the true meaning of Easter. The Crucifixion and Resurrection of Jesus Christ is the most significant religious event in the Christian calendar. Congregations gather in churches, both large and small, on Good Friday and Easter Sunday to honour these occasions.

There are more than 20,000 churches and burial grounds across England. The church itself may provide a home for mice, bats,

Above: Lesser Celandines carpet the graveyard of St John's Church at Cowgill in Dentdale, Yorkshire.

owls, jackdaws, swifts, pigeons and kestrels and the surrounding graveyard for many species of small rodents. Churchyards scattered throughout the countryside also offer wild plants a sanctuary from the effects of modern farming. Having survived for centuries, these grasses and flowers, some of them rare, merit close inspection, for they most probably indicate what England's ancient meadows must once have looked like in that particular area.

At Easter time, one of the most obvious wild flowers to look out for are the lesser celandines which brighten up road verges and peep through the grass, glinting like little golden stars in the spring sunshine. In Dorset these tiny flowers are known as 'the Spring messenger'.

Right: The hare was the sacred animal of the pagan Goddess Eostra, worshipped by our pre-Christian ancestors, later hijacked as the Easter 'bunny'.

Below: The origins of Easter egg hunts date back to pagan times.

The Growing Month of April

By the beginning of April, young shoots of corn will have emerged in straight green lines across newly sown fields and at the end of the month, rape will be bursting into flower. Oil seed rape is an annual herb which is grown extensively across Asia, Europe and Canada to produce oil for cooking and as a lubricant. It belongs to the cabbage and cress family and grows up to 5ft (150cms) tall. Sometimes it is sown in Spring but more often than not it is put in as soon as the previous crop was harvested in August or September, giving it time to grow thick and green before winter sets in. Flocks of wood pigeons find rape a very attractive winter food and can cause serious damage by stripping parts of the field bare.

Warmer weather in Spring once again triggers growth and its bright yellow flowers begin to appear in late April creating a spectacular patchwork across the English countryside for a few weeks, although the heavy scent rape emits is not particularly pleasant.

The flowers develop into long narrow pods, inside which tiny black seeds ripen; harvesting in the south of England begins in July. The stalks, which are of no use, are usually chopped and spread as they leave the back of the combine and then ploughed back into the soil.

Rape seeds readily germinate given the right conditions, and

Above left: The expanding population of wood pigeons feed on oil seed rape throughout the winter.

Above right: Warmth and moisture in April hasten the growth of Spring corn.

wherever it has been grown, rogue plants appear afterwards. These are particularly noticeable along the roadside where odd seeds have fallen from agricultural machinery and benefited from moisture running off the tarmac. Rape is quickly becoming a common weed.

Organic crops can be produced at high prices for the minority, but the use of sprays on mass-produced farm crops is a necessity. Just as flowers and vegetables in the garden suffer attack by pests and diseases, so do agricultural crops. Pesticides deal with pests such as carrot fly, pea moth and aphids. Fungicides are used to treat rusts, moulds and various other fungal problems. Herbicides control weeds.

Some of the latter sprays have been cleverly developed to selectively destroy certain plants while leaving the crop unharmed. Other types of herbicide sprays defoliate everything they touch but are rendered harmless by contact with the soil. There are also slower-acting systemic chemicals which are absorbed through the root system or leaves, killing the weed from within. Sophisticated development of safer sprays over the years means that fewer are now being used: the more effective they are, the less is needed. Modern machines are also more precise in delivering spray evenly over the crop at the prescribed rate. British fruit and vegetables supplied to supermarkets are continually monitored and stringently tested. They are virtually free of any potentially harmful residues by the time they are harvested. Anyone wishing to buy British produce should look for the symbol.

Genetic modification (GM) is viewed by many with concern but it could be used to produce crops that are genetically resistant to some diseases and pests, thus reducing the use of sprays. Millions of pounds are spent annually by the agricultural industry researching chemical use and GM experiments.

Below: By the end of April the rape flower will be creating a vibrant patchwork of yellow across the English countryside.

Return of the Wild Boar

Still widespread across Europe and Asia the wild boar (*Sus scrofa*) was once native to England but became extinct in the 17th century. A modern farmer seeking alternative ways of profiting from livestock saw a potential market and the first wild boar farm was established in Cambridgeshire in 1981. Several farmers followed suit, keeping them outdoors to satisfy the increasing demand for naturally-bred meat.

Inevitably a few escaped and during the great storm in October 1987, the full force of which hit Kent, a mass breakout took place. Consequently wild boar are now breeding in the wild, and once again inhabiting woodland in Sussex, Kent, Dorset, Herefordshire, the Forest of Dean and recently north Devon. The latter were released from a nearby farm by animal rights activists in December 2005. Serious attempts were made to recapture them but some, including pregnant sows which can give birth to as many as twelve young, quickly dispersed into the surrounding countryside. It is thought likely that there may be other isolated pockets of wild boar existing elsewhere in England.

Potentially wild boar can be dangerous for they are large animals, up to 6ft (2m) in length and weighing 400lbs (180kgs). Although they are most likely to avoid contact with humans, a female with young will instinctively defend them. Males are fearless and well-equipped to fight, should the need arise, with tusks up to 10ins (25cms) long.

In the wild they are very elusive, despite their size, for they cleverly conceal themselves during the hours of daylight. The most likely indication of their presence is tell-tale tracks, wallows and obvious places where the earth has been turned over by foraging. Wild boar are very adaptable as has been discovered in Germany where an estimated 5,000 now live in the city of Berlin.

There is huge controversy as to whether wild boar should be welcome to once again roam the English countryside. While some

conservationists are pleased to see their return after more than 300 years, others are gravely concerned about the long-term effect they will have on flora and fauna – for wild boar will eat anything, including ground-nesting birds.

The harm they can cause to plants when foraging is great although it is possible that some species may actually benefit from the soil being disturbed, allowing dormant seeds to regenerate. Farmers are worried about potential damage to crops and fences as well as being very concerned that their selectively-bred commercial pigs kept out-of-doors are at risk from disease and of being mated by roving boars.

Above: A wild boar sow suckles her young. The high value of wild boar meat has encouraged some pig farmers to switch to this species.

Opposite: After an absence of about 300 years, escaped wild boar are re-establishing themselves in the English countryside.

English Styles of Stone Walling

Stone Age man built the first stone walls 5,000 years ago and field boundaries have been marked ever since by our ancestors who used whatever material was available locally.

Ditches were dug to fill up with water in low lying areas, hedges were planted on good land, banks were sometimes built up and wherever stone could be found, it was put to good use. Probably the best known and most spectacular stone wall in England was the one Emperor Hadrian ordered to be built in AD122 to protect the boundary of the Roman Empire against barbarians from the north. Stretching 73 miles from the Solway Firth in the west to the mouth of the river Tyne in the east, it was originally 8-10ft (2.4-3m) wide and 12-16ft (3.6-4.8m) high. Forts and castles were built at intervals along its length.

Dry stone walls (built without the use of mortar) are still very much a feature across many northern and western parts of England. Each area has its own local design. There is a collection of different styles at the Westmorland County Showground near Kendal and a permanent exhibition at the National Stone Centre, near Middleton-by-Wirksworth in Derbyshire. Here the millennium was marked by the opening of a 200 metre trail consisting of 19 sections all built in one weekend in 2000 by members of the Dry Stone Walling Association in local styles from all parts of the country.

Many walls were built to mark boundaries when the Enclosures Act put a stop to common grazing in the 18th century, and still remain intact. Men were also found work stone walling during the depression of the 19th century.

In the north of England large uncut stones are used. This requires great skill in placing each stone so that it holds the others in place. Steps are sometimes built into the walls. Holes may be left in the bottom: small ones to allow the passage of rabbits and hares and larger ones, often known as 'cripple holes', for sheep. There are also two types of stile: a 'step' stile and a 'squeeze' stile, which is just wide enough for a human to pass through but too narrow for livestock.

At the other end of England, Cornish walls are built with two rows of stones with the gap between filled with soil. Plants soon take root and it is not long before the wall takes on the appearance of a solid bank playing host to a wonderful diversity of grasses and flowers.

Cotswold walls are made from the local sandstone which is softer and can be split and fashioned to give a more 'finished' appearance. Approximately 2ft (60cms) wide at the bottom, they taper to about 14ins (35cms) at the top and the gap between the outer layers of stones is filled with smaller ones.

The soil in many eastern and southern chalklands of England contains flints which, although often used in the construction of houses and barns, have never been extensively used for field boundaries, as mortar is required to bind them together.

Stone walling competitions and demonstrations provide a public display for the skills of craftsmen who build and repair a permanent feature that contributes so much character to the English landscape.

Opposite: Repairing a dry stone wall in Cumbria.

Above left: Stone walls in the Yorkshire Dales not only confine livestock but also provide shelter from the wind.

Below: Cornish walls are built with two rows of stones and the gap between is filled with soil. A multitude of plants soon become established, disguising the wall.

Breeding like Rabbits

When celebrating Easter, early Christians substituted the rabbit for the hare which the pagans had held sacred as part of their Spring festivities. Rabbits (*Oryctolagus cuniculus*) are thought to have been brought to England by the Normans in the 11th century as a useful source of food. They have the capacity to reproduce very quickly and can survive on poor forage, converting it into lean meat.

The name 'rabbit' was originally applied only to a young rabbit, a mature one being known as a 'coney'. Many centuries ago huge areas of dry unproductive land across England, such as Dartmoor and the sandy heaths of East Anglia, were made into large pens where wild rabbits were farmed for meat. These areas were known as 'warrens' which could be up to 1,000 acres (400 hectares) in size and were enclosed with high banks.

'Warren' is a place name still found across England today and is indicative of what the surrounding land was once used for. Lodges were constructed on high ground where warreners lived and watched over their stock, for poaching was rife. Even well into the 19th century, the penalty for illegally killing a rabbit was lengthy imprisonment or deportation to Australia for seven years. One of these lodges, built in the 15th century, can still be seen near Thetford in Norfolk, an area famed for its warrens. An East Anglian trade developed in the 19th century of preparing and dressing skins, a preliminary treatment in the manufacturing of felt. The rabbit pelts were then dispatched to hat-making businesses in Luton and elsewhere, and the meat was sent by train to London or Cambridge to feed the students. There were processing factories in the neighbouring town of Brandon and a little museum there explains the history of rabbit warrens in the surrounding 'Breckland' area.

The industry lingered on until the 1950s when there was no longer a demand for either rabbit meat or skins. Man-made materials began to take the place of natural fur and fibres. In 1953 the horrific scourge of myxomatosis was introduced to control the millions of rabbits which at that time were devastating much-needed food crops. The disease spread like wild-fire across the country but a nucleus of stock survived which soon began to multiply. They are very resilient animals and now there is an estimated rabbit population of 38 million in England.

Rabbits have several litters of babies each year which are born helpless, blind and naked inside a fur-lined nest underground. They are sociable animals and live in colonies but a strict hierarchy exists, with a dominant buck and doe. As well as having prodigious appetites, rabbits dig holes which, if out in the fields, can indirectly cause

Below: A single family of young rabbits. Rabbits have a well-deserved reputaton for breeding prolifically.

injury to livestock and damage to machinery. In some places they are still present in pest proportions so keeping their numbers under control is very necessary but even so, they do have their uses at times for conservation purposes.

Some species of plants and wildlife on heathlands need a habitat of bare ground or closely-cropped grass that only rabbits can create. There are certainly times when the much-vilified rabbit earns a well-deserved place in the restoration and conservation of these heathlands.

Above: Young rabbits enjoying the Somerset sunshine.

Left: In medieval times rabbits were farmed in warrens. This lodge at Thetford Warren in Norfolk was built to house the warreners employed to look after the rabbits and protect them from poachers.

63

Rooks and Crows are Hatching

Carrion crows, rooks and jackdaws, along with ravens, hooded crows, magpies and jays are all members of the crow family, commonly known as corvids.

The throaty calls of rooks (*Corvus frugilegus*) invariably evoke a sense of the countryside. They are noisy, gregarious birds and in autumn great flocks of young and old join together to share winter roosts. At dusk, several hundred may be seen gathering on fields, before settling down for the night in woodland close by. The largest rook roost in England is near Buckenham in Norfolk and was first recorded a thousand years ago in the Domesday Book.

In January, groups return to nest sites used the previous year and renovate the old nests with fresh sticks. Country lore has it that if nests are built high in the trees it will be a fine summer but if low down, it will be a bad one.

These communal nest sites are known as 'rookeries'. Three to five eggs are incubated for about 18 days and young birds usually leave the nest in early May. It was once thought to be lucky to have rooks nesting near your house but on the other hand if a single rook settled on the roof then there would be a death. "A rook on the thatch, death lifts the latch".

Landowners encouraged rooks to continue nesting on their land for they believed that if a rookery was deserted then misfortune or even death would befall their family. Many country folk refer to rooks as crows but, where they are correctly identified, rooks are generally regarded as less of a pest than crows. True, rooks gather on rubbish dumps and will take eggs, small mammals, chicks and grain, as well as damage newly-sown crops by digging up seeds and worms – but they also do good by consuming harmful grubs which infest the soil, such as leatherjackets, which are the larvae of daddy-longlegs (crane fly). Rooks have benefited greatly from the expansion of free range pig farming. By stealing food they are guaranteed a plentiful supply throughout the year. The increase in maize growing has also helped

Above: This pair of rooks have even used some orange baler-string to line their nest.

Right: The communal nesting site shared by rooks is known as a rookery.

them as they relish the newly-planted seed and the cobs in autumn. Rook pie used to appear on country menus every May when the young first left the nest and it is thought that the nursery rhyme 'Sing a song of sixpence a pocket full of rye, four and twenty blackbirds baked in a pie' may have referred to rooks. The collective name for a small gathering of rooks is a 'parliament'.

Unlike rooks, crows (*Corvus corone corone*) are solitary birds and are considered to be the worst villains amongst corvids. In Spring a pair will build an untidy nest of sticks in a small tree. It is then that most damage is done, for they systematically work their territory, raiding the nests of other birds, taking both eggs and chicks. For the rest of the year, fresh meat is their first choice which they find as road kills or from birds or animals that have died naturally. A gathering of crows is known as a 'murder'.

Jackdaws (*Corvus monedula*), smallest of the black corvids, are very adaptable rural scavengers. They can be found not only in

the English countryside but also on coastal cliffs and are well adjusted to urban living. They are cheeky birds and can often be seen on the backs of deer or sheep, searching for parasites such as ticks or collecting hair or wool for nest building. They prefer to nest in cavities, such as in hollow trees, which they pile full of sticks and rubbish. But jackdaws are at their most annoying when they choose a chimney as an alternative to a tree. If they don't manage to block the chimney with sticks (which itself can have serious consequences) then soot and twigs will fill the grate. It is amazing how jackdaws can get in and out of a chimney but not uncommon for a young one to fall down one and end up in the room, or become trapped behind a boarded-up fireplace.

Above: The jackdaw is the smaller cousin of the rook and the crow. Their thieving reputation derives from their propensity to 'steal' shiny objects.

Right: The carrion crow is famous for its intelligence. Its predatory nature can have serious consequences in the countryside.

66

Windfarms on the Horizon

Fossil fuels (gas, coal and oil) have been the principal source of fuel and power in England for decades but these resources are limited. When burned, they release harmful emissions (greenhouse gases) such as carbon dioxide (CO_2) into the atmosphere, prompting fears of global warming.

Yet, with ever-increasing demand for energy, alternatives have been sought. Nuclear power, available since the 1950s, is one option but many people are gravely concerned about the risks and long-term consequences of using radioactive material.

Some power stations use renewable resources such as wood or grasses – known as bio-mass. Bio-mass fuel also emits harmful carbon dioxide when burned, but this is to some extent compensated by the fact that when plants grow they absorb carbon dioxide from the atmosphere.

Once again making use of the natural energy of water, wind and sun are coming under close scrutiny as the most environmentally friendly way forward.

But at present less than 5% of the energy we use comes from these sources.

Surprisingly for a country surrounded by sea and criss-crossed by rivers, it is not hydro-power but wind-power that is now attracting most interest in England.

The concept of using the wind was brought back from Arab countries by the Crusaders and our ancestors harnessed its power by building windmills to pump water and grind corn. 350 windmills were still in use in 1919, but the convenience and reliability of coal, gas and oil gradually superseded them.

A new breed of windmill is appearing on the English horizon. To some they are objects of beauty, to others ugly blots on the landscape. They are expensive to erect but cheap to run, cause little noise, no pollution and there are no waste products. However, they need to be sited in places where the wind is most consistent and at its strongest.

A massive off-shore wind project is underway in the Thames Estuary, between Essex and Kent, consisting of 341 turbines. Unfortunately, most new windmills are prominently sited on land around the coast and on high ground, often in some of the most beautiful parts of England.

Single giants (217ft/67m high, with blades 100ft/31m in length) can produce enough electricity for an estimated 3,000 people, although this figure is disputed. Groups of smaller wind turbines (100ft/31m high) are collectively known as wind farms.

As farmers search for ways in which to diversify, a few wind-powered turbines on the farm can be an attractive financial proposition. Five 50ft (15m) high turbines can provide sufficient power to run a farm, with any surplus being fed into the National Grid.

Above: One of the largest wind turbines in England (275 feet high) is at Swaffham, Norfolk.

Left: A wind farm in Cornwall.

Primroses and Pussy Willow

The month of April acquired its name from the Roman word 'Aprilis' meaning opening up, and is certainly the month when the earth opens up. There is an old saying that 'April showers bring forth Spring flowers' and it is certainly a time when warmer weather and longer days seem to wake up the whole countryside.

One of the most familiar Spring flowers is the beautiful yellow primrose (*Primula vulgaris*). It is a member of the Primula family, many of which have been cultivated as garden plants. Cross-pollina-tion frequently occurs, resulting in oddly-coloured wild primroses. Its name is from the Latin 'prima rosa', meaning first rose. It is some-times called the 'Easter rose' and is the county emblem of Devon.

The primrose (*above*) is a perennial that flowers from March to May and is surprisingly catholic in its choice of habitat, appearing all over England in open woodland, on grassy banks, embankments and occasionally even on sea-facing cliffs. Our ancestors used primroses for flavouring food and in wine-making. The leaves boiled together with lard produced an ointment that was used to treat cuts and sores.

There are many different species of willow growing wild in England, some of which are known by alternative names such as

withy, sallow and osier. Sallow (*Salix caprea*) is also called 'goat willow' but is more often referred to as 'Pussy willow' or 'Palm'. The Sunday before Easter is known as Palm Sunday, a reference to the day when people were said to have thrown palms on the road in front of Jesus as he entered Jerusalem on a donkey. Pussy willow has been substituted for palm at Easter celebrations in some countries which is how it has become known locally as 'palm'. The familiar oval, fluffy, silver-coloured flowers, which quickly mature and become covered in yellow pollen, appear before the leaves.

Above: Primroses in Coverdale announce the arrival of Spring in the Yorkshire Dales.

Left: The early flowers of Sallow, commonly known as Pussy Willow.

Opposite: In country folklore primroses are associated with fairies.

Historic Buildings

Castles, stately houses, cathedrals, priories, abbeys and other historic buildings, dating back a millennium, can be discovered scattered throughout the English countryside. Some are merely ruins, but others are well preserved and open to visitors. Most castles are strategically sited overlooking river valleys or around the English coastline.

They reveal how our ancestors lived and worked and the many priceless house collections reflect the interests of past owners. These displays of wealth and the skills of the tradesmen and artists employed are truly astounding. Some of the most splendid mansions are now owned and managed by the National Trust while others are the ancestral homes of Dukes and Lords who still live in parts of the house. The upkeep expense of such places is enormous and often part-funded by allowing paying visitors to view the most impres-

sive rooms and works of art. One fine example is Derbyshire's Chatsworth House (*above*) which has been open to the public ever since it was built. Set in an estate of 35,000 acres (14,000 hectares) it is one of the most palatial stately houses in England.

The site of Bamburgh Castle (*below*) on the Northumberland coast has been occupied since the first century BC. The centre of the present castle, which sits on the top of a basalt outcrop overlooking the North Sea, was constructed during the reign of Henry II (1154-1189).

MAY

The Swanage Steam Railway running between Corfe Castle (*above*) and Swanage in Dorset was closed in 1972 and it took a band of dedicated volunteers 20 years to restore the line. Enthusiasts across England have reopened sections of many other steam railways that were axed in the 1960s. By doing so they have preserved not only the buildings, engines and carriages but also the embankments which are themselves micro-nature reserves.

Steam engines are deceptively quiet when idling but burst into noisy action when set to work. Their fiery stomachs, fed with dusty black coal, belch clouds of steam with the effort.

While it's a novelty for children to ride on a steam train, it's also a nostalgic journey for their grandparents who lived in the days when many more people travelled by train than owned a car. Thanks to the efforts of hundreds of volunteers the sounds and smells of steam engines are still with us to elicit childhood memories.

The Vixen and her Cubs

The indigenous red fox (*Vulpes vulpes*) is the only wild relative of the dog still living in Britain. For decades, fox numbers have been increasing and many now make their homes in English towns and cities. Here they do not have to kill for a living but can rely on stealing food put out for pets and garden birds or scavenging on discarded take-away meals or out of dustbins.

This is not a natural existence for a predator and many urban foxes are in poor condition. In the countryside, foxes have to hunt to live, often raiding the farmer's chickens, ducks and geese. They have the unfortunate habit of killing much more than they need, maybe taking only one or two dead birds and leaving behind dozens that they've killed or injured. Although foxes are omnivorous it is much easier for them to satisfy their hunger by killing a few birds or animals than it is to catch hundreds of beetles.

No ground-nesting bird or small mammal is safe from their attentions, especially in the breeding season when their prey is at its most vulnerable. Foxes also kill a number of new-born lambs of the smaller breeds of sheep on the northern hills and Fells, for a ewe with twins cannot protect them both. Rural folk turned a chore into a sport, so a few centuries ago tracking down the culprit developed into chasing it with a pack of hounds.

Foxes are known by various names such as 'Reynard', 'Charlie' and, in the north of England, 'Tod'. They are agile, stealthy and

May foxes, busy feeding their young, widen their hunting territory.

cunning, and their movement is more cat-like than dog. An adult fox can weigh more than 25lbs (11kgs). They are mostly nocturnal and quiet although around Christmas time, when they are searching for a mate, they become much more vocal. The scream of a vixen is a chilling sound on a frosty moonlit night.

In Spring a litter of three to seven young are born underground in a den known as an 'earth'. The vixen stays with her cubs for the first few weeks while her mate brings food but as they grow bigger, both parents will hunt for them. Occasionally another non-breeding vixen will assist with raising the litter.

Young cubs are very playful and trample the soil and vegetation around the earth with their games. When they are older their

Above: The games fox cubs play around this time of year help develop the hunting skills they will need to survive.

parents will move them to another earth or sometimes, if there is enough cover, they will live on top of ground. At this stage the cubs begin to hone their hunting skills by catching worms or beetles and in autumn the family splits up. In winter foxes grow a thick coat and look much fatter than they do in summer. There may be quite a variation in colour: some foxes are a light sandy brown, some red, while others are much darker. White markings on the chest are not uncommon and sometimes even occur on the feet. Contrary to country lore neither the size of a fox nor whether or not it has a white tip to its brush (tail) gives any indication of its sex.

Silage Cutting Begins

The weather in May is generally warm, the soil still moist and the days long – all of which encourages rapid plant growth.

There are 150 different grasses in England and certain high-yielding species have been developed to provide good grazing. Some grass fields are set aside in Spring to be harvested later to provide winter feed for livestock.

With the advent of mechanisation it became possible, in the early 1950s, to preserve fresh grass as silage. This was a blessing for farmers as it made storing good quality winter fodder less of a lottery and very much easier.

Grass for silage is usually cut in May, before it gets too coarse. It is left a day or two to wilt before either being packed tightly into plastic-covered bales out in the field, or taken back to the farm loose in trailers. Now is the opportunity to incorporate additives such as molasses, to improve the food value. Then it is heaped up in a 'clamp' and firmly pressed down before being covered with sheets of plastic which are often weighted down with old tyres.

Over the following weeks the green grass naturally ferments to produce silage, a nourishing and palatable feed for cattle and sheep. Fluids slowly seep out and great care has to be taken that this effluent does not enter waterways because it is very harmful to fish.

As grass in the fields continues to grow throughout the summer another later cut may be taken.

Silage-making starts in May, while the grass is still tender.

Hard Times for Sheep Shearers

Above: It takes an experienced shearer about a minute to shear a sheep. Shearers wear felt slippers to prevent slipping.

From May in the south of England to July in the north, sheep are normally sheared for their own well-being. On upland farms it is a major undertaking to gather the semi-wild sheep off the hills or moors, so hill farmers sometimes band together to help each other out.

Farms with large flocks often employ experienced contractors who can each shear up to 300 sheep a day. Some members of these shearing gangs may well be from New Zealand, a country renowned for lamb and wool production, who seek employment in England when it is winter in their home country.

It is very important that the wool is dry when it is clipped. The fleece holds together as it is skilfully sheared off close to the skin with mechanical clippers. It is spread out on a clean surface with the clean, inner part uppermost, then rolled into a bundle. Wool is naturally greasy and 'lanolin', a sticky yellow oil used in the preparation of cosmetics, is extracted from it.

Originally sheep were kept for their milk but when the Romans invaded England they brought with them their own breeds of sheep to improve the wool quality. Wool production in England had become very important for sheep farmers by medieval times and many small villages in East Anglia and the Cotswolds boast disproportionately large churches built on the riches of the wool trade. The importation of cheap wool from Australia and NZ, and today's modern synthetic fleeces, have resulted in a collapse in demand for wool, and meat has become the prime source of income.

Britain now produces a mere 5% of the world's output of wool. There are 60 breeds of sheep and 100 grades of wool. Lesser grades of fleeces are virtually worthless and the cost of shearing and transport now outweigh the value of most grades. New regulations have made the disposal of unusable fleeces difficult as they can no longer be burned, so other uses are developing, such as house insulation or horticultural mulches.

75

The Wild Flowers of May

In a recent poll, the bluebell (*Hyacinthoides non-scripta*) was voted the most popular flower in Britain. Bluebells grow from a bulb and are a member of the lily family. It is probably one of the most easily-recognised of English flowers and the UK is home to half of the world's population. Occasionally a pale pink or white flower may occur naturally.

Bluebells are distributed right across the British Isles and if undisturbed will remain *in situ* for hundreds of years. Great swathes carpet many damp but well-drained deciduous woodlands beneath ash, oak and beech trees. Bluebells can also be found growing in the open on upland grasslands and occasionally sea-cliffs. When coppice work is carried out in woodland, they are one of the first dormant plants to come to life.

In many places conservation groups such as the Woodland Trust permit the public to access bluebell woods in May especially to enjoy the sight and scent of nature's most beautiful springtime display. As sunlight filters through the freshly opened leaf buds of overhead trees and spotlights the expanse of vivid blue beneath, the spectacle is almost magical.

Folklore has it that you could summon fairies by ringing blue-bells. In the past the bulbs were used in herbal remedies, as a fabric stiffener and to make glue. But they are now fully protected and it is against the law to dig them up. All is not well though as in some places our native bluebells are under threat from cross-pollination from the more robust, cultivated Spanish variety which has been dumped in woods. It is estimated that one third of our bluebells are now either Spanish or hybrids.

The bluebells at West Woods, Manton, near Marlborough.
Half the world's population of bluebells grow in the UK.

77

Above: Welsh poppies growing wild against a Cumbrian dry stone wall.

Left: The delicate flowers of the wood anemone, often found in the blue-bell woods.

The wood anemone (*Anemone nemorosa*) is a poisonous member of the buttercup family and because the dainty flowers appear to dance in the breeze, it is sometimes called the 'windflower'. They are common in deciduous woods on well-drained soil and often carpet the ground in May.

If you spot clumps growing on mountain ledges and in hedgerows and on banks, this indicates that the area was probably once woodland. Although appearing to be white in colour, the backs of the flowers are tinged with pink or purple and the stamens are pale yellow.

The Welsh poppy (*Meconopsis cambrica*) is not confined to Wales and can also be found growing naturally in moist shady places, especially in the south-west of England. This delicate yellow flower has long been a favourite in cottage gardens from whence it escaped and it has now become naturalised in some areas. This pretty poppy can be seen in May brightening up the narrow verges of twisting Cumbrian roads around Coniston.

Dairy Herds in the Meadows

The majority of milking cows are kept in the west of England where higher rainfall and milder winters ensure a plentiful supply of grass. A large cow may eat as much as 150lbs (70kgs) of grass in a day.

Modern trends have favoured commercial herds of black and white Friesian or Holstein cows which yield a lot of milk with a low percentage of fat. Medical experts have encouraged us to have a more healthy diet with reduced fat consumption, so dairy farmers have acted accordingly. In fact they can now be penalised for supplying milk that has too high a percentage of butterfat.

As well as cream and cheese, milk is also used to make yoghurt, butter and tinned dairy products such as custard and milk puddings. While many English counties are famous for their local cheeses, it is for clotted cream that Devon and Cornwall are best known.

The local breed of South Devon, known as 'Ruby Reds' are large animals and were once dual-purpose, being kept for their rich milk and for meat. However, these days they are more likely to be eaten in a Cornish pasty than milked, as they are now favoured for producing succulent beef.

Both Jerseys and Guernseys are renowned for their rich creamy milk but these pure bred herds are now few and far between and are likely to be kept specifically for the production of cream or ice cream. Jersey cows are small, light-framed animals, only two-thirds the weight of the much bigger Holsteins. Guernseys are slightly larger than Jerseys.

These Channel Island breeds only produce about two-thirds as much milk as Holsteins but what they do give is very rich, with the butterfat content a third higher and, being smaller animals, they do not cost as much to keep.

The famous Devon and Cornish Clotted cream is made by leaving the milk to settle for twelve hours which allows the cream to rise to the top. The cream is skimmed off and then slowly heated to a high temperature but not allowed to boil. This process allows a thick crust to form. The top layer is again skimmed off, potted and cooled which makes the crust on top harden and the cream beneath thicken. The high carotene level in the lush West Country grass gives clotted cream its distinctive yellow colour.

Above: Jersey cows in Cornwall. Famous for their rich, creamy milk, Jerseys are no longer a common breed on English farms, due to the current trend for a low-fat diet.

The Helston Flora Dance

Many villages celebrate the arrival of Spring on 1st May with dancing around a maypole, but nowhere in England is it celebrated in such spectacular fashion as in the Cornish town of Helston.

The roots of the town itself go back a long, long way to pre-Saxon times. In 1066 the Manor of Helston was held by Harold, Earl of Cornwall who that year became King of England only to be defeated by William the Conqueror at the Battle of Hastings shortly afterwards. The first of 24 Royal Charters granted to the town was proclaimed by King John on 15th April 1201.

Helston is famed for its Flora Day and Furry Dance. As with so many Spring festivals, the celebrations are pagan in origin and may well have once taken place on 1st May when the first day of summer was marked with the Beltain festival. However, Flora Day now takes place on 8th May unless it falls on a Sunday or Monday, in which case it is celebrated on the previous Saturday. Streets and houses are decorated with bluebells, gorse and greenery.

The processional dancing is formal, covering several miles. Each procession follows the Helston Town Band with the first dancers setting off in pairs through the streets at 7am. Just before ten o'clock, up to a thousand local school chil-

Above: Helston Flora Day begins at 7am with the first dance.

Left: Up to 1,000 local school children join the dance, school by school.

dren, aged five to seventeen, begin their dance. Each child is dressed in white, girls with coloured flowers in their hair and boys with ties to denote their school. As they finish, more adults set out. Leaving the Guildhall precisely as the town clock starts to strike 12 noon, the men are all formally dressed in top hat and morning suits and the women in elegant long dresses, dancing around the town and through some shops and houses. They are representative of the gentry who once lived in Helston while the early and late dancers (another group sets off at 5pm) portray servants who were only allowed to join in before and after their work.

Above: The Hal-an-tow celebration at Helston, Cornwall, is reminiscent of a Pagan festival.

Another celebration – the Hal-an-Tow – begins at 8.30am. This re-enactment of rustic pagan rituals involves a rowdy crowd of men and women, old and young, dressed in costumes, carrying banners and blowing whistles, processing through the streets. From time to time they stop to read out a proclamation and sing the Hal-an-Tow song. To be at Helston on Flora Day stirs a sense of taking part in some very ancient ritual.

Nesting Waders

A rare visitor to England every Spring is the sparrow-sized Little Ringed Plover (*Charadrius dubius*) often seen close to water, either on river estuaries, seashores or reservoirs. However, it occasionally chooses to nest a little way inland where the ground is sandy or gravely. Similar in appearance to its cousin, the resident Ringed Plover, it is slightly smaller and can be identified by a yellow rim round the eyes. Its eggs are laid around May in a scrape on the ground lined with small stones or pieces of chalk. Both parents take turns to incubate them.

Perhaps the most evocative sound of Spring and summer, across the open moorlands of northern England, is the plaintive, bubbling cry of the curlew (*Numenius arquata*) as it calls out its name. It is largest of the waders found around our shores and marshes and moves inland to nest on open moorland and some-

Top: Little ringed plover chicks shelter from the wind beside their mother.

Above: An oyster catcher sits tight on her exposed nest in the driving rain.

times even in lowland areas. The curlew's long, down-curving bill enables it to probe muddy or boggy places for invertebrates and marine molluscs.

The nest is little more than a scrape in the ground in which four large eggs are laid. Incubation is shared between both parents and takes about four weeks. The chicks are active soon after hatching.

Another wader to occasionally forsake the coast or lake shore and move inland to nest is the oystercatcher (*Haematopus ostralegus*), a striking black and white bird with a long orange bill and red eyes and legs. Its nest is just a scrape in the ground, lined with small stones, often in an exposed position. Three or four eggs are laid which are well camouflaged. The parent birds are identical and, because of their colour, are very conspicuous when incubating eggs. If there is any danger they will quietly leave the nest and try to attract attention away from it, often by feigning injury.

Oystercatchers nesting inland almost seem to celebrate when their young are fledged and strong enough on the wing to return to the sea or lake shore, for family groups can be seen flying low overhead, calling shrilly as they pass by.

Above: A young curlew chick is very soon running around.

Below: The babbling cry of the common curlew is always a pleasure to hear on the open moors and rough meadows in Spring.

Coppicing and Charcoal Burning

For centuries people prized woodland as much as they did open grassland. Trees and shrubs provided them with nuts and berries, firewood, tools; and the plants that grew beneath them were sources of food and medicine.

The woods also furnished people with a home and a living, making baskets, fencing, charcoal, in fact a multitude of things. By taking a harvest from the woods they created a mosaic of habitats in which a diversity of insects, mammals, birds and plants survived.

Many different species of trees were coppiced in rotation. Sweet chestnut was used to make fencing; hazel for wattle and gate sheep hurdles; willow for baskets; and ash for tools. Other species such as oak would be left to grow bigger so it could be cut for timber and used for making beams, posts, furniture or boats. Every tree in the forest had a specific use.

Coppicing was a common practise in which wood was cut after the leaf had fallen and before the sap rose again in Spring. The summer was spent making up the products. Without the shady canopy of leaves blocking out the light, plants that had lain dormant in the forest floor would come to life. The stools (stumps) would soon sprout several new shoots up to 6ft (2m) high in the first summer. After 5 to 20 years, depending on the species and use it would be put to, it could then be cut again.

Coppicing played an important part in the ecology of any deciduous forest but as the practice died out during the last century, so our woodlands and the flora and fauna within them deteriorated. So many animals, birds, butterflies, moths, bees and other insects are dependant on different habitats within a forest. Woodland conservationists now recognise the value of coppicing to create greater bio-diversity and are reintroducing it as part of their management programmes. The old art of charcoal-making is being revived, using the surplus wood. The traditional method of making charcoal was in large circular iron kilns, some of which are still being used. Rusting

Top: The old art of charcoal production is being revived. Its production benefits English woodlands.

Above: As soon as woodland is coppiced, plants that have been lying dormant burst into life.

remains can often be found in old woods. Unwanted timber that has been left to season is cut into manageable lengths then stacked inside and a fire is lit at the bottom. Six tons of hardwood are needed to produce one ton of charcoal. Either a lid or turfs are placed on top to control the rate of burning. The wood inside is left to burn very slowly for up to three days.

This results in complete carbonisation of the wood which then needs to cool for 24 hours before it can be taken out, graded and bagged. British charcoal produced in this way does not need firelighters or fluids and very soon gets up to temperature. Local production not only benefits our own woodlands but reduces the associated environmental problems that go hand-in-hand with foreign imports. Charcoal was once used extensively in furnaces for the iron industry and for the last 700 years has been mixed with potassium nitrate and sulphur to make gunpowder.

Above: Mark Harris, hurdle-maker, at work in a Dorset wood. A traditional hurdle-maker would be kept in continuous work on about 14 acres of hazel woodland, coppiced in rotation.

Forest Parks and Cycling

The State-owned Forestry Commission, through its agency Forest Enterprise, is responsible for managing about one quarter of England's woodlands to which the public have access. Bridleways and walking trails are very well marked and in some places picnic sites and children's playgrounds are provided. Camping, caravan sites and cabins are even available in a few areas.

Some of the forests have excellent visitor centres attracting thousands of visitors throughout the year. There are car parks, shops, restaurants, barbeque facilities, picnic tables, disabled access and miles of tracks leading out into the forest. For a modest charge to park the car, these Forest Centres offer a day out in the country-side that can be enjoyed by all ages and abilities.

A seat in the sunshine, a leisurely browse round the gift shop and a cup of tea in the café may be sufficient for those who merely wish to relax. Young children can be kept amused for an hour or two climbing, sliding or swinging in the play areas. Marked trails of different lengths make walking a pleasure and for those seeking more of a challenge, there is orienteering with specially prepared maps available and well-marked points.

The ultimate daring adventure, however, is to pay for a session on the 'Go Ape' high wire forest experience where crossing rope bridges, swinging tarzan-like between trees and descending zip slides at speed are all options! Forest Centres regularly hold wildlife, educational and activity events especially for children during school holidays; and on certain dates during the summer, outdoor concerts

Above: The 'Go-Ape Experience' at High Lodge, near Thetford, Norfolk offers excitement high in Forest Enterprise's trees.

attracting well-known performers take place.

Cycling in Forestry Commision land is also available on the safe, designated tracks. Typically, sites such as High Lodge Forest Centre near Thetford in Norfolk has 25 miles (30km) of well-marked off-road bike trails. Bicycles of all sizes can be hired, some with little trailers attached so that even the youngest member of the family can enjoy the ride.

In the last few years an initiative to make cycling in England safer and more pleasurable has been set up with the formation of the 'National Cycle Network' which is co-ordinated by the sustainable transport charity 'Sustrans'. It extends to more than 10,000 miles (16,000km) and about a third of the network consists of traffic-free paths. The remainder is on quiet country lanes or little-used urban roads. Dedicated cycle lanes have also been put in beside busy roads and countryside off-road trails follow canal towpaths, forest tracks and disused railway lines.

There can be much more to visiting a forest than just looking at the trees.

Below: Forest parks offer safe, off-road cycling for all the family.

Above: Roe deer fawn. Baby deer are deliberately left hidden in undergrowth or fields of grass by their mothers and should not be touched or picked up because this might cause parental rejection.

JUNE

Before silage-making became so prevalent, the grass in meadows was allowed to mature and not mowed for hay until June or July. It was then left in the field to dry naturally. In good weather the crop might only need turning once before being raked into rows and picked up or baled. This traditional method of farming allowed flowers and grasses time to seed, naturally re-establishing themselves for the following year.

However, when there were showers or prolonged periods of rain, as often happens with England's fickle climate, the hay-making process would be lengthy, mowed grass would become mouldy and the quality deteriorate until it was of little value; which is why farmers now prefer to make silage. This has destroyed most of our ancient pastureland but fortunately some traditional hayfields have survived, such as Yellands Meadow in the Yorkshire Dales (*above*) which is now carefully preserved by the Yorkshire Wildlife Trust.

The Appleby Horse Fair

Many centuries ago a royal charter was granted to hold an annual Fair at Appleby-in-Westmorland (now in Cumbria). Originally it was held in the town centre but around 1750 the site for selling horses, cattle and sheep was moved to Gallows Hill, a field one mile north of the town, which was subsequently renamed 'Fair Hill'.

Appleby Fair is held in early June and is now confined to the sale of horses and ponies which are brought along by travellers and dealers. It became a somewhat low-key event in the mid-1900s but the last 30 years have seen a revival in its popularity. Once again it has become a major event in the diary of travelling people across the north of England. It is an annual pilgrimage for some of the surviving genuine Romany gypsies. Although greatly outnumbered by shiny chrome-clad modern trailers, horse drawn wagons still wend their way along the surrounding country roads before gambling with the dangers posed by modern transport on the last perilous few miles along the A66 to reach Appleby.

Times have changed and few gypsies still live a life 'on the road' in horse-drawn wagons, for it is no longer so easy or safe for them. But for those living in houses, the yearning remains and the two or three weeks spent reaching their Mecca is regarded as a holiday. Some of these true Romanies are people of means and own busi-

nesses but the urge to travel with a horse and wagon still pulses through their veins just as wild birds instinctively migrate. They are immensely proud of their splendid coloured cobs and their beautifully-decorated wagons. These few are joined by an assortment of other wagons and carts, some very simple, and not always driven by genuine gypsies but by those who are tempted to 'live the dream'.

Several hundred caravans gather on the hill for the Fair. It is a chaotic place where travelling folk meet up, where deals are done, where horses are shown off and young lads and lassies do the same. Although the Fair is held on the outskirts of the town, the centre of Appleby is bedlam during the few days the gypsies and travellers are visiting. Many of the youths, riding bareback at speed, take their horses and ponies down to the river where they wash and swim them through a deep pool by the bridge. Local roads also provide an ideal place to exhibit the pace of trotting horses which can reach a speed of 30mph. With such a disorderly mix of horseflesh and humans in such close proximity, a visit to the Fair may prove slightly hazardous.

Similar gatherings are also held twice yearly in May and October at Stow-on-the-Wold in the Cotswolds.

Opposite and above: Gypsies washing their horses and ponies in the river Eden at Appleby.

Right: Some gypsy wagons are elaborately decorated.

Far right: On their way to Appleby Fair.

Salad Days and Strawberries

Although machines have been invented to do most things, certain crops still need to be carefully gathered by hand. Obviously this is very labour intensive in England and sufficient local helpers aren't often now available. Gangs of foreign migrant workers, however, have been willing to come to England to do the sometimes tedious job of picking summer crops.

At this time of year, salad onions and young carrots are usually pulled and bunched on the field before being put into crates for transporting. Watercress, herbs and salad leaves such as rocket are picked then taken to packing sheds where they are sealed in plastic bags to keep them fresh. The sorting and packing of some crops such as iceberg lettuce, cauliflowers and celery is carried out inside huge

Opposite: Most English strawberries are picked by gangs of seasonal workers – many from countries within the newly expanded EEC.

Above: Picking salad leaves on a farm near Thetford in Norfolk.

machines which creep slowly across the field. Soft fruits need to be picked by hand although there is now a machine that will collect blackcurrants.

The very popular strawberry is a member of the rose family and is propagated from plants growing on runners thrown out from the parent plant. Tiny little strawberries grow wild in the English countryside but the familiar fruit now farmed commercially originates from America. Strawberries are known to have been cultivated by the Romans as early as 200BC and in medieval times they were regarded as an aphrodisiac. Mixed with borage and sour cream it was customary for them to be served to newly-weds at their wedding breakfast. In the past many strawberries were grown on the outskirts of London to be sold in Covent Garden Market.

Perhaps the event now most associated with strawberries is the Wimbledon Tennis Championships where about 2 tonnes are consumed each day, *Elsanta* being the most popular for flavour.

The season when fresh fruit is available has been extended by the use of polytunnels, but mid-season crops are still often grown in the ground outside and are obviously very dependant on fine summer weather. Straw is usually spread around each plant to raise the fruits off the ground to keep them dry and clean.

Beef Calving Timed for Lush Grazing

The production of beef has entered several different phases during the last century. Prior to the 1940s, England's local breeds of cattle could commonly be found in the counties where they originated. Some were dual-purpose animals kept for milk and meat such as the Red Poll from East Anglia, Lincoln Reds, South Devons and Shorthorns. Some breeds – Jerseys, Guernseys and Ayrshires – were kept specifically for milk production. Others, such as the Sussex and Hereford, were of little use for milking, but they were inclined to fatten quickly so they were kept for meat.

After the Second World War the trend was to produce food quickly and cheaply. This meant that smaller, faster-maturing beef breeds which were weaned early and housed indoors such as the black Aberdeen Angus became popular.

Then came the demand for leaner meat with a higher proportion of best quality cuts. This brought about the introduction of breeds from the Continent carrying much more flesh on their hind quarters, which provide steaks and the best roasting joints. The first breed to become popular was the cream-coloured Charolais, imported from France in 1961, but others like ginger-coloured Limousins, pale red and white Simmental and the grotesque blue and white Belgian Blues have since become very much in demand.

The latest phase of beef production has arisen from public demand for more naturally produced food and consequently there has been a move to keep beef cattle out-of-doors for most of the year. The combination of all these trends has resulted in the wonderful variety of coloured animals that can now be seen grazing in the English countryside.

The cows are frequently of mixed breeding and calving is often timed for the Spring or early summer when there is plentiful grass. Bulls from one of the Continental breeds are often left running with the herd of cows and their calves all summer. The youngsters aren't weaned until late autumn by which time some of them appear to be almost as big as their mothers. They are either sold as 'stores' for someone else to finish fattening or housed in barns until they can be turned out again in Spring. The cows too will often also be kept inside for the winter.

Beef is best 'hung' (matured) in a cool place for three or four weeks as this process helps to improve the texture and flavour.

Limousin bull

Simmental bull

Red Poll bull

Opposite: Belgian Blue and calf. The well-developed hindquarters of this calf show why this breed produces plenty of steaks and good joints for roasting.

Above: Beef bulls are often turned out with cows and their calves.

Bees Harvest the June Nectar

It is estimated that 80% of our food crops are pollinated by bees. There are about 250 species in England but the most useful of these to humans are honey bees (*Apis mellifera*) for not only do they pollinate plants but they also produce honey and bees wax.

Honey bees can only survive as a colony which consists of a single queen (the sole sexually-reproductive female); drones which are male; and workers which are naturally-sterile females. Each serves a different and very important function.

The whole colony circulates around the queen who can produce as many as 3,000 eggs a day. She is fed a substance called royal jelly produced from a gland on the heads of worker bees. Drones have only one purpose and that is to mate with the queen. Within a few days of a queen hatching and setting up a new colony, she will be mated. This takes place on the wing 300 or 400 feet (100m) up in the sky. The drone will then die. A queen may be mated several times in the course of a few days but that is sufficient for her to remain fertile for the rest of her lifetime.

In autumn the workers stop feeding any surviving drones, leaving them to die. The queen can control the fertilisation of her eggs. Unfertilised ones become drones while fertilised eggs develop into female workers or sometimes other queens.

Workers construct cells of two sizes, the larger ones for drones. The queen walks over them and knows which sort of eggs to lay where. When a hive becomes overcrowded the workers decide that more queens are needed to set up new colonies and so they build special cells in which the existing queen can lay her chosen eggs. These special larvae are then fed exclusively on royal jelly. The development of a queen from an egg through the larva and chrysalis stages takes 16 days, a worker 21 days and a drone 24 days.

The honey bees we commonly see (and sometimes get stung by) are workers, of which there are tens of thousands in a colony. They secrete wax from glands beneath their stomachs to build honey-

Above: The bee collects nectar in a sac attached to the oesophagus and then gathers pollen on its hind legs.

Below: Worker bees on the honeycomb. The elongated cells are occupied by developing queens.

Right: Conservation measures which increase the number of wild flowers will also help the diminishing population of bumble bees.

comb. One ounce (28g) of wax is strong enough to hold four pounds (1.8kg) of honey. Workers gather nectar, pollen and water which they convert into honey. In addition to looking after the queen, her offspring and making honey, workers truly live up to their name by keeping the hive clean and maintaining the constant temperature of about 98°F needed within the nest for eggs to hatch. If the weather is cold they gather together to maintain warmth and if extremely hot they will fan the eggs with their wings to cool them.

Once hatched, the larvae require frequent feeding with royal jelly for a couple of days and then with pollen which is pure protein. Should the larvae develop into workers during Spring or summer their lives will be busy but short, perhaps only lasting six weeks. Late-hatched ones will survive the winter for although they don't hibernate, they're not active when it's cold and have little to do except keep warm.

Workers start their lives as apprentices before going on to do more important jobs such as comb-building and feeding the larvae. It is the most mature workers who are responsible for fetching nectar, pollen and water. They forage in a radius of up to three miles. When a worker discovers a newly-found source of nectar, it will communicate this to the other bees when it returns to the hive through a complex ritual of dancing, indicating the distance and position in relation to the sun. Bees feeding on rape or heather flowers have the reputation for being aggressive.

When a new queen hatches, the old one will leave the colony with half the worker bees to establish a new one. Apart from when she is mated it is the only time a queen ever leaves the hive. The swarm may settle in a chimney, a hollow tree, on a branch or even in the nearby post box to establish a new colony. Most are collected by bee keepers and an old adage has it that 'A swarm of bees in May is worth a load of hay, a swarm of bees in June is worth a silver spoon but a swarm of bees in July isn't worth a fly'.

Bee survival is at the mercy of many things. Woodpeckers and mice raid hives and the Varroa mite sucks blood from larvae resulting in them being weak, deformed and susceptible to viruses. Harmful crop sprays once took a heavy toll but fortunately this particular problem is now being addressed.

Busy Time for the Bee Keeper

Without bees we would be short of food, for it is mainly bees that fertilize flowers, enabling them to develop into seeds or fruits. But the benefit from bees goes far beyond that function, for man discovered many thousands of years ago that they also produce honey and wax. Honey gathered from the wild was used as a sweetener long before sugar became widely available; and mead, made from water, honey and yeast, has been a popular alcoholic drink for centuries.

Early bee keepers devised a method of controlling bees by keeping a swarm in a simple 'skep' made out of woven straw which could be kept in cellars during the winter. At one time honey was an acceptable way of paying the rent. Wooden hives came into use towards the end of the 19th century, making managing bees and collecting honey much easier.

A hive is divided into two parts: a brood box at the base with vertical frames where the queen lives and breeds; and shallow boxes above called 'supers' where the honey is stored. Each frame consists of a foundation sheet of a paper-thin layer of honeycomb-patterned wax on which the bees can build their comb. A screen separates the two compartments allowing only the smaller worker bees access to the 'supers'.

Each hive houses a colony of several thousand bees leading a very complex lifestyle revolving around a single queen whose sole purpose is to continuously produce eggs which develop into larvae. By day pollen gathered from flowers is carried on the hind legs of bees and nectar is collected in a sac attached to the oesophagus. On the bees' return this is regurgitated into the mouth of a young worker within the hive and deposited into a cell in the brood box. Overnight any surplus nectar, not needed to feed the young larvae, is moved in the mouths of workers from the bottom chamber to the 'supers' above. Enzymes in the saliva react with nectar to make honey.

Weather, more than anything, determines production as it not only affects the bees' activity but also the flowers, for a certain

Bee keepers (apiarists) checking their hives.

JUNE

98

amount of warmth is needed before nectar is released. Unless the moisture content of the nectar stored is reduced to between 15% and 17% it will ferment, so young workers fan the comb with their wings to reduce the moisture. Once honey in the supers is ripe, then workers seal it over with wax.

Bee keepers collect this honey at least twice during the summer although honey gathered from rape flower sets quickly and mustn't be left for very long. There is little nectar available for the bees after August. All honey is liquid when it is first produced. The wax cap the bees use to seal it with has to be removed with a knife. It can then be extracted from the frames by being gently spun in a drum, throwing it to the sides. The honey can then be run off into a container. An exception is heather honey which is too gelatinous to be spun in this way so it has to be pressed out instead.

Once extracted the honey is then filtered and stored in small buckets. This then has to be warmed slightly before being poured into jars to sell. On average each colony of bees can be expected to produce over 30lbs (13.5kg) annually and sometimes honey is offered for sale still in the comb. All honey will eventually granulate although at different rates according to the source of nectar. The process can be hastened by the addition of 10% set honey and the colour depends on which plants the bees have visited. After separa-

tion the cappings from the comb are warmed then cooled so that they solidify and can be separated and any last honey drained off. Finally, the wax is heated, poured into moulds and allowed to set once again. Some is used to make the very thin sheets which are slotted in each frame within the hive as a foundation for workers to build on. The rest goes to making such things as cosmetics, polish and of course candles.

The medicinal and antibacterial properties of honey have long been recognised and today honey is still occasionally used to treat infected wounds in hospitals. Another product obtained from bees is propolis, a brown sticky substance which also has antiseptic properties. It is collected from the buds of plants and used by bees to seal gaps in the hives. Slugs, caterpillars and even mice that enter the hive and are too large to be removed, are stung to death by the bees and encased in propolis to prevent contamination within the colony.

Below left: When the comb is filled with honey the bees cap it with wax which has to be removed before the honey can be extracted.

Below: The comb is melted down and the wax used to make cosmetics, furniture polish and candles.

Below right: The Bee Boles at the Lost Gardens of Heligan. Before waterproof hives were made, bees were kept in 'skeps' made from barley straw housed in alcoves known as 'boles'.

The Stoat and the Weasel

Most people find it difficult to tell stoats (*Mustela erminea*) and weasels (*Mustela nivalis*) apart. This is hardly surprising because they are both small animals and often a fleeting glimpse is all that is seen of them. They are similar in colour and shape, but a stoat has a black tip to its tail and is nearly twice the size of a weasel.

Around June, playful young stoats may be seen following their mother in a long line, nose to tail. They stay together as a family for several months, a fact which probably gives rise to the frequent debate as to whether stoats hunt in packs.

They are blood-thirsty little carnivores taking mice and voles and they regularly hunt and kill prey much bigger and heavier than themselves such as fully grown rabbits and young pheasants. They can also climb well making use of ivy growing on trees and walls to take young birds from their nests. Stoats are active both day and night and invariably kill their prey by biting the back of the head where it joins the neck. They are not popular with country folk for they have the habit of killing more than they eat.

Stoats have only one litter a year, usually in April or May, which may number as many as a dozen. They are a distant relation of the badger, and like them they mate again soon after giving birth but the fertilised egg lies dormant for many months inside the female.

Once development is triggered in the early Spring the actual gestation period is between three and four weeks.

In the cooler temperatures of the north of England stoats generally turn white in winter but keep the black tip to their tail. This fur is known as ermine from which the robes worn for State occasions by peers of the realm are made. In the south, stoats normally remain brown although perhaps turn a little darker in their winter coat. In between these areas it is not unusual to find partially coloured stoats in winter. They are common and widespread and can be found in any kind of habitat from sand dunes on the shore to the Fell tops.

The smaller weasel is also widespread across England, and although it is one of our commonest carnivores it is seldom seen. It too will tackle prey much larger than itself but generally catches mice, field voles and young rabbits. Being so tiny, weasels are able to follow them through their network of underground tunnels. Weasel populations fluctuate depending on the breeding success of their prey. They are very agile and have been known to raid tit nesting boxes for chicks, as they are small enough to get inside through the entrance hole.

Weasels are prolific breeders but unlike stoats there is no delay in the development of the fertilised egg. The first of their two litters each year, of up to eight young, are usually born in late March after a gestation period of about five weeks. Weasels will sometimes make use of an old nest of their prey species which they line with fur. Survival rate is not high, for they themselves are prey to owls, hawks and cats. Weasels were once tamed and kept for pest control in the home and, like stoats, were believed to hunt in packs.

For centuries they have been attributed with magical powers and have been variously referred to as 'dandy dogs', 'mouse hunters', 'canes' or 'minivas'.

Left: The stoat has a black tip to its tail. It is a ferocious little hunter.

Above: The weasel is about half the size of the stoat and, although quite a common English mammal, it is a rarely seen.

Cuckoo and her Helpers

By early June, tiny host-parent birds all across England are busy feeding their monstrous foster cuckoo chicks. In fact, the cuckoo (*Cuculus canorus*), one of our best-known summer visitors, proclaims his arrival from mid-April onwards. The familiar sound heralds warmer days to come and when first heard is always worthy of comment. It is only the male who emits the repetitive call, either on the wing or perched in a tree.

Despite its familiar voice, the cuckoo is not easy to see and can very easily be mistaken for a hawk flying overhead. Having spent the colder months in Africa, cuckoos return to breed in England, and they are unique in being Britain's only parasitic bird. They manage to conduct themselves in a very clever way and while a male is busy announcing his whereabouts, his mate is quietly seeking out nests of other birds in which to lay her eggs. Remarkably she not only concentrates on one particular species but she also matches the colour of the eggs she lays to those of the host bird.

Even though they are widespread, fewer cuckoos are returning to England, possibly corresponding with a decline in the numbers of their host species. Cuckoo eggs are laid in the nests of many different birds but their favourites are the dunnock (hedge sparrow) in woodland, meadow pipits on moorland and reed warblers in wetlands. Their small eggs are laid singly in each nest, although in total a cuckoo may lay more than twenty. The egg needs to be incubated for about twelve days and, once hatched, the chick soon evicts any other eggs or chicks from the nest. It grows very quickly, fledging in about three

weeks, after it has increased its size 50 times. In fact it grows so rapidly it's not able to remain in the nest for all that time. Perched just above, it waits with its beak in a wide yellow gape in anticipation of food from any passing bird. This sometimes works, for another parent carrying food for its own young will mistakenly stop to feed it. Cuckoos will often eat furry caterpillars which other British birds treat with disdain.

Above: A meadow pipit at the entrance to her well-disguised ground nest. The species is often targeted by the opportunist cuckoo.

Opposite: This reed warbler has its work cut out feeding a voracious cuckoo chick, already more than twice its foster mother's size.

As summer progresses adult cuckoos become less vocal and usually head back to Africa at the end of July. Incredibly, youngsters follow later in September using only their natural instincts to find their way. It used to be thought that cuckoos remained in England for the winter but changed into hawks.

Many other things that coincide with the appearance of cuckoos have been gifted with its name. Cuckoo-spit stuck on plants contains the baby of a small insect known as a frog hopper. Cuckoo bees use the same parasitic breeding techniques as cuckoos for a queen invades the nest of another bumble bee, kills the queen and then lays her eggs there, leaving the host workers to rear her offspring.

Mid-summer Wild Flowers

Many ancient grass meadows were ploughed up after World War II so that cereals and quicker-growing varieties of grasses could be planted. The old meadows would also have been full of wild flowers so it is lovely to see them once again making an appearance, putting on a glorious show in late June.

The introduction of conservation headlands (field perimeters) on arable land started the process in the 1990s and it was incredible how plants responded to an absence of agricultural sprays.

The first and most obvious to appear on the field margins were bright red poppies whose seeds had lain dormant in the soil for many years. It is thought that poppies were growing in England more than 5,000 years ago when the first Neolithic people cut down trees to farm the land. Ceres, the Roman goddess of corn, is depicted wearing a wreath of poppies and in medieval times they were known as 'corn roses'. Poppies were never picked, as superstition had it that there would be violent thunderstorms if they were. Red poppies have become the poignant symbol of Remembrance Day because during the First World War at Flanders and other battlefields, constant shelling disturbed huge areas of earth and poppies grew there in profusion afterwards.

Several agro-environmental schemes have been implemented throughout England in recent years and in order to reduce food production, fields are put into 'set-aside' meaning that they are left uncultivated for one or more years. The land can't be ploughed but must be left unplanted unless sown with a non-food crop that is beneficial to wildlife. Set-aside land can be sprayed with herbicide after 15th April but may not be cut until after the 15th July. The Stewardship Agreement allows farmers to grow wild bird feed plots to utilise odd corners of fields.

Yellow corn marigolds, red poppies and blue cornflowers were once common weeds found growing in fields of corn.

They are also permitted to plant wild flower mixes which benefit a whole range of insects. The seeds of once-common annual arable 'weeds' such as blue cornflowers, pink corncockles and golden corn marigolds were not as resilient as the poppy, and have required the farmers' intervention to make a come-back.

In restored meadowland, many species of butterfly will seek nectar from the mix of flowers. So too will bumble bees which, unlike honey bees, live in small colonies and usually build their nests in the ground. There are 24 species living in Britain but their numbers are in decline. Many other small insects (which birds need to feed their young) are attracted to the plants, so the knock-on effect of growing these wild flowers benefits a whole range of wildlife. Farmland bird numbers have declined by more than 50% since the 1970s but agro-environmental schemes have halted the decline and since the 1990s numbers have stabilised and some species are on the increase.

Below: Poppy seeds can lie dormant in the soil for many years. New environmental schemes encourage farmers not to spray around the edges of fields and as a result many poppies have reappeared in cornfields.

The Very English Allotment

Allotments first came into being in Victorian times when workers left the countryside to work in factories, moving into long rows of terraced houses with no more than a yard at the back. Times were hard so growing food not only helped eke out their meagre income but reconnected workers with the land.

However, the allotment really came into its own during the last war when in the 1940s Britain was very short of food as shipping was constantly under attack. The 'Dig for Victory' initiative gave families the incentive to do their bit. One and a half million allotments came into use and many gardens were turned over to vegetable growing. Food rationing didn't end until 1954.

When things began to return to normal, allotments became neglected and were devoured by building projects. But now there has been a resurgence of interest and demand for allotments is increasing. The Allotments Regeneration Initiative (ARI) has been set up and a National Allotments week is held each August to promote them.

Below: Well-tended allotments at Youlgreave, Derbyshire.

JULY

Formed more than 75 million years ago, the Seven Sisters cliffs between Seaford and Eastbourne (*above*) are a well-known landmark. Two belts of undulating chalk hills lie south of London. The North Downs extend 95 miles from Farnham in Surrey to the English Channel near Dover, while the South Downs stretch 90 miles from Winchester in Hampshire to Eastbourne in East Sussex. Here they literally tumble into the sea, for chalk is very unstable, sometimes eroding more than 12 inches (30cms) a year. Beachy Head at 575ft (175metres) is the highest chalk cliff in Britain. Separating these two sections of coastal cliffs are low-lying reclaimed areas of the Pevensey Levels, Walland and Romney Marshes. Chalk is a soft marine limestone, accumulated millions of years ago from algae, micro-organisms and the skeletons of sea creatures. Hard grey flints are also often found in chalk deposits and appear as narrow level bands running across the fragile cliff faces. At their base, shingle beaches, formed from Ice Age flint, are constantly rearranged along the shoreline by the relentless sea.

Steaming July

Each July sees one of the biggest gatherings of steam age monsters from the past at Weeting in Norfolk. Here and at the Great Dorset Steam Fair at Stourpaine every September, these lovingly preserved relics from the past are shown off. Many hours are spent by their proud owners polishing the paintwork and brass in preparation. Children wonder at the machine's gigantic proportions while grandparents reminisce about pre-war days when they could see them at work, for it wasn't until the 1950s that the last steam traction engines were retired from active service.

The basic workings of a steam engine are quite simple. Coal is used to heat water in a cylinder which forms steam. The pressure of this is used to work a piston. This in turn can be fixed to a wheel from which a belt is attached to another implement. The first crude steam engine was invented at the end of the 17th century but it was during the 1800s that steam power changed people's lives forever. In 1814, engineer George Stephenson began experimenting with building steam locomotives and, working with his son, unveiled his famous 'Rocket' in 1829, forerunner to our steam passenger service.

On land the 19th century was truly the age of steam, enabling man to have previously unknown power at his fingertips. Gigantic traction engines were used for powering rides at fairgrounds and more importantly for ploughing, threshing and pulling heavy loads. Local contractors would hire themselves and their machines out for farm or road work and a wagon would be towed behind in which the operator lived while he was away from home. But within the decade

Below left: Traction engines disappear under a pall of smoke at a steam rally at Weeting.

Below right: A last-minute polish.

Steam engines powering threshing machines were once a common sight before the advent of combine harvesters.

of the 1950s, just as steam railways were beginning to disappear, so too were the gigantic steam traction engines.

Fortunately, many have been preserved and restored by collectors who appreciated the magnificence of these great machines. Some are individually owned while others are part of impressive collections. One man who could not bear to see them neglected and rusting away was the late George Cushing MBE from Thursford in Norfolk where many immaculate machines associated with steam are on display at his museum. Another large collection can be seen at Hollycombe near Liphook on the Sussex/Hampshire border. Several other places have a few on display and sometimes steam traction engines and road rollers appear at country fairs.

Deer Farming for Venison

In mid-summer, a red deer hind will normally give birth to a single calf, which will continue to suckle naturally for about seven months. Red deer (*Cervus elaphus*) are the largest of the six species of deer found in England and are native to this country.

You can spot wild red deer herds in several places including the New Forest, Norfolk and particularly on Exmoor. Female red deer are large animals and generally have a placid temperament which is why they have proved the most suitable species to farm.

Only stags (males) have antlers which in successive years grow bigger until the stag is about seven years old by which time he will be in his prime and may weigh nearly 29 stone (180kg). Antlers grow fresh each year. At first they have blood circulating through them and are covered in soft skin called velvet. In some countries this velvet is collected for export to the Far East as an aphrodisiac. After a few months the antlers are fully developed, blood circulation ceases, the velvet peels off and the antlers become rock hard. Red deer cast their old antlers in late winter and will often chew on them to top up their calcium levels.

For safety reasons, when they are confined in paddocks, stags running with the herd usually have their antlers removed for they can cause serious injury to each other as well as humans. Once the antlers have become hard they no longer have any feeling and can be sawn off without causing any pain to the animal.

For most of the year, wild red deer live peacefully in single sex herds but during the rut (mating season) in October the hormones rage. Stags develop thick necks and seek out the hinds announcing their presence with a groaning roar. With only one thing on their minds they continually round up their harem and become very aggressive towards other stags.

Venison is a very healthy meat, low in fat and high in iron and other necessary minerals. It is increasingly offered for sale in supermarkets, shops or farmers markets and served in pubs and restaurants. It is most often sourced from deer kept in captivity although some is culled from the wild.

Although not strictly farmed in the true sense of the word, venison also comes from the smaller fallow deer (*Dama dama*) that can be found in many of the parks surrounding stately homes. They are semi-wild and live and breed naturally although they

Above: A red stag closely guards his hinds during the rut.

Opposite: Herds of fallow deer are frequently kept in parkland surrounding grand mansions.

Below: Red deer calves, like all baby deer, are kept hidden for the first few weeks and a spotted coat provides good camouflage.

are confined within a very large area. This grassland has probably never been ploughed or fertilized and fallow deer from these parks are therefore totally free range and almost organically produced although they may require supplementary feed in winter.

In such a protected environment numbers naturally increase by more than a third each year, so selective culling is necessary. Numbers need to be kept under control as there is a limit to how many deer an enclosed area can support. Fallow deer in Britain died out during the last Ice Age but were re-introduced by the Normans for hunting.

Remnants of these ancient wild herds remain in many places including the New Forest, Epping Forest, Richmond Park and Cannock Chase. Fallow vary in colour: some which are pure white have been selectively bred over many generations from the more common darker coloured specimens.

Irrigation and Water Management

At the height of a summer drought, fields everywhere become parched. Ears of corn don't fill out, root crops don't swell as they should, grass stops growing and turns brown. Marshy ground and heavy clay land can usually bear the brunt of a drought but not so ground best suited to growing salad, vegetable and root crops which is of necessity light, free-draining land that doesn't retain water.

Being able to irrigate on a large scale has enabled modern farmers in drier parts of England to produce crops where it had previously been impossible. During the last century licences were issued permitting farmers to drill bore holes on their land to tap into underground water supplies. Inevitably demand for water for agricultural and domestic use increased and it has become obvious that underground supplies are not limitless. Water has become a valued commodity.

Consequently during the last decade there has been a switch to storing water for crop irrigation in huge purpose-built reservoirs sited on the farm. These are dug out, lined with a heavy duty lining and surrounded by a bank of earth. They can then be filled during the winter with surplus water pumped from nearby rivers once they have reached a certain level. However it is a costly investment and farmers can't afford to irrigate all their crops, only those which are of maximum importance and most likely to suffer.

Sugar beet and cereals are usually left to take their chance, nor is it economic to water grassland so stores of winter fodder may have to be ransacked to feed livestock when hot sun and lack of rain has scorched the grass. Delicate salad and herb plants cannot survive drought but require a gentle method of watering so fine sprinklers are used. These automatically progress their way from one side of the crop to the other although some are designed to work in a circle from a central pivot.

'Rain guns' which spray water from a large oscillating hose and are automatically dragged back across the field and rewound onto a gigantic reel are used on the more robust root crops such as potatoes and carrots.

Above left: A man-made rainbow as a potato crop benefits from irrigation during a spell of dry weather.

Below: Sugar beet wilts under a blazing sun but is usually left unirrigated.

Sussex Trug-Maker

Nearly every large village in England once had a basket-maker and whatever grew locally would be used in its making, even rushes. Willow, which is also known as osier or withy, has long been a basket-making favourite and is still most widely used. Young growth is cut while it is still pliable enough to be woven and basket-makers of old sat on a flat board on the floor to weave the willow. On the marshy Somerset Levels, common osier grows along the drainage ditches known as '*rhynes*' and is regularly pollarded. For centuries these willow trees have been cut back to about six feet above the ground, just beyond the reach of cattle. New shoots or withies sprout from the top of the trunks and are harvested every few years.

In Sussex, the white or cricket-bat willow (*Salix alba caerulea*) is used to make trugs. The word 'trug' is derived from 'trog' an Anglo-Saxon word meaning a boat-shaped wooden vessel. They were originally made in different sizes for measuring grain or liquid. Now they are useful baskets for gathering vegetables and flowers in the garden or can be put to more decorative use, filled with potpourri or

Above: A Sussex trug being made at the truggery near Herstmonceux

Below left: Trugs of all sizes

flower arrangements. The craft of trug-making has been established in Sussex for more than 200 years where they are still made in the traditional way. The rim and handle is made from sweet chestnut with the bark left on. This is split with a cleaving axe and then smoothed with a 'drawer-knife'.

After it has been steamed, the strips become pliable and are bent round wooden 'formers' to acquire the shape needed. Lumps of well-seasoned cricket-bat willow, that have been left to dry out for several months, are sawn into thin planks of the required lengths. The trug-maker sits at an ingeniously designed wooden 'horse' which holds the wood firm while he works on it. Each plank is then shaved smooth with the drawer knife. After being dipped in water, which makes them flexible, they can be curved into shape and nailed to the frame with copper pins.

In Cumbria a bent hazel rod is used to form the rim and handles for baskets made from thinly split coppiced oak. These are known locally as 'swills' and before the invention of plastic, swills were used for a variety of purposes around the farm including carrying peat or charcoal.

JULY

113

Water Voles Fight for Survival

A 'plop' in the water is often the first indication of the presence of a water vole.

In warmer weather it is often possible to get a good sighting of a water vole (*Arvicola terrestris*) from paths beside some of the rivers in Derbyshire and even in villages and towns such as Shrewton and Warminster in Wiltshire. Even where there is a lot of human activity it is surprising how tolerant these amusing little creatures have become.

They are the UK's fastest declining mammal and conservationists are working hard to counteract the decrease. There are many reasons why the survival of beloved 'Ratty' of *Wind in the Willows* fame, has been threatened.

Water voles are entirely aquatic vegetarians. They can't survive for very long without water and in a very dry summer, when the ditches and streams where they have made their homes dry up they are forced to move. This is more marked where there are chalk streams for here rainfall may take several months before it permeates the land and the streams can disappear even after fresh rain. The number of water voles has declined by 90% in the past 60 years but in many areas where they have disappeared, re-introduction is now taking place. Schemes have proved successful in places such as the London Wetland Centre and on the Avon and Kennet canal.

The destruction and fragmentation of their habitat has increasingly become a problem. Water voles have many enemies including rats, stoats, dogs, owls, hawks, herons and even pike. The biggest though is the presence of carnivorous North American mink which have flourished since being both accidentally and deliberately released from fur farms in the past. They find water voles easy prey.

Where mink have been successfully eradicated by river keepers wishing to protect their stocks of fish, there are still thriving populations of water voles.

The water vole is the largest British vole, easily told apart from rats by their blunter faces and shorter tails. They are active both day and night, and often the first indication of their presence is a 'plop' as they dive into the water. Water voles live in burrows in banks. If these are surrounded by short grassy 'lawns' where they have been feeding, it is a good indication that the holes are occupied. They store food underground for the winter although they do not hibernate.

Water voles are usually very unsociable towards each other, although females still manage to produce several litters of five or six young between March and October. Generally their survival rate is poor but given the right conditions they can quickly regenerate.

Above: If the grassy bank above a burrow looks like a mown lawn, there is probably a resident.

Left: Water voles are aquatic vegetarians.

How to Spot a Woodpecker

There are three species of woodpeckers in England. Their sharp beaks are very strong and used like a chisel. The skull has shock-absorbing properties where it joins the beak and is specially strengthened to withstand the impact of hammering on hard wood. Woodpeckers eat grubs, seeds, fruits and nuts. They have very long tongues, slightly barbed and covered with sticky saliva, which they use to delve for insects and invertebrates. When not being used, the tongue is retracted into the back of the skull. Long sharp claws enable them to cling to branches and tree trunks and their flight between trees is undulating. Woodpeckers also depend on old and decaying trees for nest sites, excavating a hole at least 10ft (3m) above the ground.

The black and white Greater Spotted Woodpecker (*Dendrocopus major*) is the most numerous and widespread. Both sexes have a bright red patch beneath their tails and the male also has a red patch on the back of his head which the female lacks. Juvenile birds have a red cap. They spiral up tree trunks and use their rigid tails to balance themselves against the tree.

The call of a greater spotted woodpecker is a sharp 'chack' and in Spring they hammer persistently on a hard dead branch to mark territories and attract a mate. This reverberating drumming carries long distances. Up to six eggs are laid and both parents share incubation which lasts for 17 days. The chicks are fed on solid food and sometimes even the chicks of other small birds are brought for them. In fact this species can be quite persistent in raiding tit nest boxes. The lesser spotted woodpecker is similar in appearance but smaller, much rarer and seldom seen.

The green woodpecker (*Picus viridis*) is often called a 'yaffle' which is a good description of its laughing call. It is the largest of our three woodpeckers and is beautifully coloured in shades of green

The male Greater Spotted Woodpecker (left) has a red patch on the back of his head, while a juvenile (right) temporarily has a red crown.

with a yellow rump. The sexes are very similar although the male has a narrow crimson line beneath its eyes. Green woodpeckers are often seen on the ground probing the short grass of parks, gardens and golf courses in their search for ants which they extricate with their long sticky tongues. They are scarce in the north but quite common in the south and prefer deciduous woodland. Sometimes their nests can be located by the noisy welcome the chicks give their parents when they return with food.

Green woodpeckers do not drum in the way greater spotted woodpeckers do but make a slower tapping noise as they search dead wood for food. Any nuts they find are wedged into a crevice and hammered open. New nests holes are drilled each Spring but are often taken over by jackdaws or starlings. Another serious 'evictor' is the green parakeet, a foreign species which is colonising several areas in the south of England. The green woodpecker and the greater spotted are frequent visitors to bird tables, most often seen clinging to wire feeders and prising out the peanuts.

Above: Greater spotted woodpeckers are frequent visitors to bird tables.

Below: A Green woodpecker searches short grass for ants.

Alarming Wildlife

Most naturally-occurring poisons in England come from plants and fungi. Although animals don't normally touch yellow flowered ragwort (*Senecio jacobaea*) every year a few horses and cattle die as a result of eating it. It quickly becomes established on pastures and waste ground. Ragwort is sometimes called 'canker weed'. This very common plant is extremely dangerous both in its green state and dried if it has got mixed in with hay. Striped cinnabar moth caterpillars (*Callimorpha jacobaeae*) feed on ragwort without harm but through the toxins they ingest, they themselves are distasteful to birds. Yellow with black stripes is nature's way of warning that something is best avoided.

The only seriously poisonous creature in England is the adder (*Vipera berus*) although bites are very rarely fatal. There are three species of snakes in England: the adder, or viper as it is sometimes known; the grass snake; and the smooth snake. The slow worm is often mistaken for a snake, but is not one. They are all timid and non-aggressive although the adder uses venom to kill its prey. Snakes regularly cast their skins as they grow and these can sometimes be found still intact. They enter hibernation in October or November and emerge as early as February if there is a mild spell, when they can be found sunning themselves on a sheltered south-facing bank. Although adders have been known to hibernate in bogs, for the rest of the year they prefer dry places such as heaths, as do smooth snakes although they are only found in the south of England.

Grass snakes (*Natrix natrix*) however, although they can be found on chalkland and heaths, prefer to inhabit damper

Cinnibar moth caterpillars soon strip the leaves from poisonous ragwort.

places close to water and are excellent swimmers. Their diet consists of amphibians such as tadpoles, frogs and newts as well as mice and small birds. Grass snakes are widely distributed and are sometimes found in gardens. The female is larger than the male, sometimes reaching more than 4ft (120cms) in length. Mating takes place soon after they have emerged from hibernation. Adders and smooth snakes give birth to about a dozen live young in August but in contrast the grass snake lays 20-30 eggs some time between June and August in a warm damp place such as a manure heap or compost heap. Hatching takes six weeks or longer depending on the temperature of the place in which they have been laid. Grass snakes defend themselves by hissing and striking but they are harmless. Their principle defence if they are picked up is to discharge the contents of their cloacae and anal glands, producing a most unpleasant stench that remains on the clothes and hands for days.

The slow worm (*Anguis fragilis*) although looking like a snake is actually a legless lizard and is by no means as lethargic as its name implies. They are widespread and frequent drier habitats including gardens and hedgebanks. Slow worms only grow to about 12 inches (30cms) in length and feed on insects, worms and small slugs which makes them a great asset to gardeners. They retain their eggs until they are fully developed and six to twelve needle-length babies are born in August or September.

There are also two other species of lizards to be found in dry places and three species of amphibious newts which frequent damp areas and ponds. Like snakes they are all cold-blooded and hibernate in winter.

Top: Although it looks like a snake, the slow worm is in fact a legless lizard.

Above: The eggs of grass snakes may be close to hatching in July, in warm, damp heaps of vegetation all over England.

Below: The adder is England's only poisonous snake.

Conserving the Chalk Downs

Much of southern and eastern England from the Yorkshire Wolds to the Dorset Downs has chalk at varying levels beneath the ground. Chalk downland was created 5,000 years ago when Neolithic farmers began to clear the woodland that covered the country. Previous inhabitants have left a legacy of ancient grass-covered burial mounds and white symbols carved in the turf to expose the underlying chalk.

The feet of millions of sheep that for centuries grazed the downs have grooved the steeper banks into tiered sheep trods. Beech and ancient yew trees watch over deep sunken tracks worn away by feet, hooves and wheels over hundreds of years. Little flint villages and isolated cottages lie hidden in the folds of the downs.

Downland is the oldest man-made habitat in England and its quiet locations, tucked away from the bustle of modern life possess a timeless quality. In the shallow soil that covers the South Downs, as many as 40 different species of plant have been counted in one square metre of the dense springy turf. Wild thyme, harebells, orchids, quaking grass and sheep's fescue are abundant and along with other chalk-loving plants, support many insect species. The downs offer prime habitats for butterflies, snails, meadow pipits and skylarks and were once dotted with tiny grassy mounds made by yellow field ants.

Thousands of chunky little South Down sheep grazed the open grassland preventing scrub and coarse grasses taking hold. Much of this ancient habitat has been lost for ever to the plough but in 1992 an attempt was made to restore the downland round Beachy Head near Eastbourne. Some areas were cultivated and re-sown with the seeds of fourteen wild flower and grass species collected locally. Grazing with sheep and cattle plays an important part in the conservation plans. Although most of the cattle today are of mixed breeding, some pure-bred Sussex can still be found. These are believed to be descended from cattle which once inhabited dense forests growing on the heavy clay of the Weald between the North and South Downs. They were much used as draught animals to plough, pull carts and drag timber from the forest. Old photos show them yoked together pulling wagons and ploughing.

The chalk downs are dry places with no springs or streams but livestock still needed water and little man-made ponds can be found scattered across the tops of the South Downs. Mysteriously it is very rare for them to dry up, even in the hottest, driest summers. These ponds were probably dug hundreds of years ago and lined with impacted powdered chalk or clay. They are commonly known as 'dew ponds' although it is thought they are most likely to be fed by sea mists which periodically roll in from the coast rather than the formation of dew. Dew ponds can also be found in Wiltshire and Yorkshire where they were sometimes bonded with straw to make the bottom and sides waterproof. They are certainly an interesting phenomenon but many have been neglected and allowed to fall into disuse and once grasses and rushes invade the pond, their roots penetrate the waterproof lining.

A Sussex saying has it that if you can see the downs clearly, it is going to rain. On such days as these the view inland from high points such as Devil's Dyke and Ditchling Beacon, near Brighton, are absolutely magnificent.

Above: Man-made dew ponds retain water all year, a haven for wildlife.
Opposite: The carefully managed South Downs.

Cricket and Willow

On a summer Sunday afternoon, the essence of rural life across England is surely a cricket match being played on the village green. It helps to bind a community together at a time when so many activities seem to tear them apart. Pride is something sadly lacking these days but there is still rivalry between local villages and a batsman or bowler who has helped conquer the visiting side gains great satisfaction from his good performance. The origins of cricket are obscure but, like golf, may well have begun when shepherds used their crooks to hit a ball using two wooden sheep hurdles as wickets.

Today, rules of the game are complex but apply as much to village cricket as international test matches. There are 11 in a team and the wickets are 22 yards apart. Some very odd terms are used: fielders' positions are described as 'silly mid on', 'leg slip' or 'square leg', the ball when it is bowled may be a 'googly', an 'off spin' or a 'yorker' and six bowls make an 'over'.

The person batting may score a 'duck' (no runs), a 'four' when the ball rolls over the boundary or a 'six' when it sails over without touching the ground. He can be dismissed by being caught, bowled out, run out or 'lbw' (leg before wicket).

Many women now play cricket but this is not a new thing for they were playing as long ago as the late 1700s.

The hard round cricket ball has been made in the same way since the 1700s with a core of cork and latex over which red leather is stitched. English ash wood is often used to make both the three stumps and bails which are balanced on top.

Quality cricket bats are made from native willow trees. Several species of willow grow in England ranging from low-growing shrubs to trees nearly 100ft high. It is a white willow hybrid, known as Cricket-bat willow (*Salix alba caerulea*), which is used to make bats.

The trees are felled when they are between 15 and 20 years old and the timber is cleft rather than sawn into lengths. It is shaped after having been well seasoned for

Opposite: The sheep outnumber the spectators at this village cricket match in the village of Gayton.

Below: Village cricket skills may not match county standards, but there's no shortage of enthusiasm and pride.

Above: Native willows, destined to make cricket bats, growing beside the river Box on the Essex/Suffolk border.

several months, drying out and hardening so that it doesn't warp. The handle is made of cane spliced into the blade and then bound with strong Irish linen thread or layers of rubber. Off-cuts can be used for trug-making or firewood and the bark for tanning. Interestingly willow bark has long been valued for its medicinal qualities which were known to the Greeks and Native Americans. It contains the active compound 'salicylic acid' from which one of the most useful analgesics, aspirin, is derived.

Above: The Chalk Downs of South-East England. Dark chestnut-red Sussex cattle graze near the meandering river Cuckmere on its way to the sea at Cuckmere Haven, once the site for many smuggling activities.

AUGUST

In late August, purple heather flowers across the moors. After the last Ice Age most of the English landscape was covered in woodland. Then Stone Age man began clearing trees to farm the land and this, inevitably, resulted in erosion. The exposed soil of the uplands deteriorated and became sour, altering the landscape to that which we see today. These open moors in England can be found in the West Country, Peak District, Lake District and the Pennines where it is most extensive. Moorland is treeless and consists mainly of heathers, mosses, grasses, rushes, sedges and occasional scrub. Man has long utilised the moors for grazing hardy cattle and sheep. During the last three hundred years he has also shot some of the wild birds that live there. A mosaic of different stages of growth on the heather-covered slopes around Stanhope in County Durham (*above*) is indicative of how the moors are managed. Many moors also provide catchment areas from which water companies top up their reservoirs and the Countryside Rights of Way Act now permits access for walkers to many tracts of open ground.

Harvest Time

The first combine appeared in England in about 1926 but it wasn't until the late 1950s that they finally replaced the horse-drawn binders. The combine harvester integrates several operations within one machine. Corn is cut by blades at the front and is swept inside where the grain is separated from the straw which is then discharged from the back. In the early days the grain was run off into sacks but in modern machines it is stored inside a tank which, when full, is emptied into a trailer driven alongside. The very early combines only cut a width of 6ft (1.85m) but over the years they have become larger and larger and are now up to 30ft (9.25m) wide.

The corn cannot be cut when it is wet so even if it isn't raining the farmer has to wait for the morning dew to dry before he can start. In a hot summer, progress is swift and crops can be harvested when they are at their best. However, in unsettled weather every opportunity has to be taken when it is dry enough and may mean working well into the night. Combining is very difficult in showery weather. To be stored without coming to any harm, the moisture content of grain has to be no higher than 15%. In a wet summer this often means the corn has to be dried until reaching this level, an expensive procedure.

In the south of England, combining usually begins with barley and rape crops in mid-July. Wheat is the most valuable grain and the best quality, known as milling wheat, is used for bread and flour production. Continuous wet weather in August, when it can't be harvested at the optimum time, results in wheat left standing in the field becoming black with mould and even sprouting in the ear. Not only does this mean it will require drying but it will be of inferior

Left: Getting in another round of wheat before the next shower.
Below: Most straw is used for animal bedding.

quality and only fit for animal feed. Tight margins mean that cereal farmers can ill-afford the extra cost of drying.

The best barley goes for malting although most is used for animal feed. Other cereals grown less extensively are rye which is used in the food industry and oats for breakfast cereals and animal feed. The seeds of rape are crushed to make lubricants and also very healthy cooking oil which is high in omega 3. Production units are also being set up to convert rape seed into bio-fuel for motor vehicles. Occasionally, a pale blue hue is cast across the fields of England where crops of linseed are grown. The linseed flowers only bloom when the sun shines. Linseed is also known as flax and is one of the oldest cultivated crops. Oil from the seeds has industrial uses and the residue goes for cattle food while fibre from the stalks can be used in the manufacture of paper, linen and material. Crops of peas and beans are also grown for livestock food production.

Working Farm Dogs

Several breeds of dogs are particularly useful in the country-side. Terriers are fearless little creatures and excellent vermin controllers. They will kill rats, mice and rabbits and let the farmer know where a fox is laying up. In autumn and winter, gun dogs such as labradors, retrievers and spaniels provide valuable assistance flushing and retrieving game for those who go shooting. But by far the most useful working partnership has always been that which develops between a hill shepherd and his sheepdog.

For centuries this type of dog has been used to help drive livestock. They were predominantly black in colour and the name 'collie' is thought to have derived from 'col', an Anglo-Saxon word meaning charcoal. Black and white rough-coated dogs of a similar ilk were recorded in the 11th century. Until mechanised transport became available in the 20th century, cattle and sheep were driven for many miles, sometimes hundreds, across England to better grazing or to markets. Every drover had a dog or two to help him along the way, not only to herd livestock but also to catch a rabbit or a hare for the cooking pot.

Most English shepherds' dogs are border collies, so-called because they originated from the English and Scottish borders. There is also the very capable Welsh sheepdog although Bearded, Old English, Scotch and Shetland sheepdogs are unlikely to be seen working these days.

The thickness and length of a sheepdog's coat varies considerably: some border collies are very shaggy while others are smooth. The latter obviously keep cleaner but lack the advantage of a thick coat to protect them from the weather. Although black and white predominates, there are tricolour sheepdogs which have tan markings on the head and legs; and also red (brown) and white.

Above: Hill shepherds could not manage without the help of a sheep dog.

Right: A collie keeps an eye on the sheep it is working.

The collie is invaluable on open Fells and moors, with its ability to cover huge tracts of ground searching out and gathering sheep which are difficult to see among the bracken or on a far distant hill. The dogs can get to places a man can't and they also come into their own in winter when snow piles into drifts several feet deep, covering sheep which have sought shelter from a wall or gulley. Here the dog, which usually works by sight, will rely instead on his refined scenting powers to detect buried sheep. Frequently a shepherd's dogs are the only company he has all day when out on the hill and the empathy they share is more than just that of man and dog.

It would be impossible for a hill shepherd to take good care of his sheep without his canine assistants. By fixing its gaze on the sheep it is 'working', a collie has an uncanny power over them. It is interesting to see at sheepdog trials just how some dogs can control their sheep purely by 'eye'. This powerful dominance is the legacy of centuries, from the time when wolves preyed on livestock. Even today this instinctive fear of canines remains in sheep.

It is by no means only farmers who appreciate a collie's talents. Their agility, intelligence and obedience are put to good use for not only do they excel in obedience competitions but also as mountain rescue and search dogs. They are also popular pets but a collie is never happier than when it can follow its natural instincts to work.

Left: Jane Murray inspecting her freshly-made ewes milk cheese at Poppylot Farm in Norfolk.

Below: The Great British Cheese Festival, held annually at Cheltenham, offers visitors the chance to taste and buy over 1,000 different British cheeses.

Opposite right: A chance to try a piece of fine Cheddar from Quickes of Devon.

The Cheese-Maker

It is thought the art of cheese making began in 5,000 BC when early nomadic tribes used bags made from the stomachs of goats or sheep to carry milk. These naturally contained rennet, a vital ingredient in cheese-making. Until recently, when a substitute was found, rennet had to be extracted from calves' stomachs.

Although there are variations, the basic process is the same for making all cheeses: approximately one gallon (4.5 litres) of milk is needed to make 1lb (450gms) of hard cheese. Special cultures called 'starters' are added to trigger the process and the milk is slowly warmed to a certain temperature. Rennet, which contains enzymes, is then added causing the curds to set. This is then sliced into small cubes allowing surplus liquid (whey) to separate and the whey is then drained off. After being left to settle for a short time, salt is added to the curd which is then milled and any flavouring etc added.

Hard cheese is pressed into moulds and left to mature. The traditional round shape is known as a truckle. During the latter

AUGUST

stages, the character of cheese is developed in complex ways including how it is handled, what flavourings are added and the length of time it is left to mature in an environment where the humidity and temperature are carefully controlled. It is sampled by using a 'cheese iron' to extract a plug from the centre. Smoking slowly over wood shavings and sawdust can add a further dimension to flavouring.

The famous Cheddar cheese was originally stored in Somerset's Cheddar Gorge caves and Double Gloucester is made from full cream milk while Single Gloucester is made from semi-skimmed. Mild cheese will be kept for about three months and strong cheeses for up to 24 months.

Soft cheeses are not pressed and may be kept for as little as three or four weeks and semi-soft for slightly longer. Blue cheese is produced by adding blue mould spores (*Penicillium roqueforti*). After being left for a few weeks to begin the maturing process, the cheese is pierced with stainless steel needles, allowing air to penetrate which activates the blue mould and creates veins inside.

Stilton acquired its name in the 18th century from the Cambridgeshire town of Stilton which was a staging post on the Great North Road between London and Edinburgh. The unique blue cheese was sold at 'The Bell Inn' although it was actually supplied by a Mrs Frances Pawlett who lived near Melton Mowbray.

There were only 126 cheese makers remaining in 1945 but with an ever-increasing interest in the diversity of home-produced English food, especially cheeses, small enterprises producing hand-made local cheeses have become established across the country.

Whilst cow's milk is utilised in the making of most cheeses, goats and ewes milk is increasingly popular and there are a few large commercial herds and flocks supplying milk to manufacturers. Varieties and flavours are infinite and many of the innovative men and women specialising in hand-made cheeses even keep their own livestock to produce the milk they need.

Living near Rodents

There are several species of rodent in England, many of which are rarely seen; some because they are quite rare and others because they are predominately nocturnal. Rodents play a very important role in the countryside for they are food for owls, birds of prey, foxes, weasels, stoats, snakes and many other predators.

Mice are generally vegetarian, very agile and can be extremely destructive. The grey House mouse is familiar to many who lived in old houses or have outbuildings. Also very common is the Long-tailed Field mouse (*Apodemus sylvaticus*), also called Wood mouse, and a sub-species, the Yellow-necked mouse. Field mice are often unwanted winter visitors to houses, sheds and barns and will invade bee hives.

The reddish-brown Harvest mouse (*Micromys minutus*) is the smallest of our rodents and has become rare in many places through loss of habitat. Its nest is built above the ground in plants or hedge-row shrubs and constructed from hay which is woven into a ball. Conservationists sometimes try to encourage Harvest mice to nest by putting out old tennis balls for them.

The Dormouse, more squirrel-like than mouse-like in its behaviour, is rarely seen for it is nocturnal, lives in thick hedge-rows or small woods and goes into deep hibernation in winter. Its cousin the Fat or Edible Dormouse, also sometimes known by its Latin name of *Glis glis*, is not native to England but a population has become established in the Chilterns after having been released in Hertfordshire in 1902. They are a protected species.

Voles have blunter noses than mice, are vegetarian and extremely important in the food chain. Although they are normally prolific, in a poor breeding year the knock-on effect is that birds of prey, which greatly rely on them, do not find sufficient food for their

A harvest mouse uses its prehensile tail as a fifth foot.

Top: Bank voles are common but rarely seen.

Above: Rats live in the countryside but move closer to buildings in winter

Below: The Wood mouse, or aptly-named Long-tailed Field mouse.

chicks and consequently have a poor year themselves. Voles can soon bounce back, sometimes reaching plague proportions, but it takes longer for bird of prey numbers to recover. Besides the larger Water voles there are Field (or Short-tailed) and Bank voles (*Clethrionomys glareolus*) which are very similar in appearance but, as their names imply, they are found in different habitats.

Rats inhabit English towns and countryside alike and are generally regarded, with good reason, as destructive creatures. They are notorious for carrying disease and causing extensive damage.

There are two species in England. The Black rat was once the most common, but is now found only in isolated pockets near certain seaports. Brown rats (*Ratus norvegicus*) are abundant across farmed areas and in summer when food is plentiful they live in tunnels dug in the ground. In winter they move closer to buildings where they can find stored grain or wasted livestock food. Their versatility is the key to their success. Brown rats will eat anything including live birds and small animals, eggs, plants and discarded human food. Rodents of all kinds pay secret night-time visits to bird feeders where they gather up seeds and nuts to cache away.

Common, Pygmy and Water shrews can be recognised by their flexible pointed snouts but they are not rodents. Rather they are carnivores, feeding on insects and invertebrates. Shrews are among our oldest surviving mammals. They are tiny hyper-active creatures which need to consume their body weight each day, therefore needing to feed very frequently. Predators such as cats and foxes kill shrews but don't eat them because the flesh is tainted by scent glands on their flanks. Their saliva also contains toxins. Weighing only a quarter of an ounce (7.5gms), the Pygmy shrew is the smallest British animal.

Red and Black Grouse

'The Glorious 12th' heralds the beginning of the grouse shooting season this month, although it is September before many estates make a start. It is said to have been called 'Glorious' since Henry VIII, who preferred hawking to politics, passed a decree that the Royal Counselors' vacation should start on the first day of the grouse season, August 12th. For many years after 1531 it was the day that the royal court's council broke up for its summer recess.

Red grouse (*Lagopus lagopus*) are a sub-species of the Willow grouse found across Scandinavia and Russia and the Willow ptarmigan of North America. Red Grouse are both indigenous and unique to Britain. They are generally considered to be the ultimate sporting game bird. Grouse require very careful management for they are truly wild birds. Sufficient breeding stock needs to be maintained but, if there are too many, they don't thrive.

A pair of Red grouse requires about five acres (2 hectares) of well-managed moorland to support them and territories are hotly defended. The grouse season extends until 10th December and only the surplus is shot each year. In a poor breeding year, shooting is cancelled. Heather forms the major part of their diet and the survival and breeding success of Red grouse depends greatly on heather management to provide different stages of growth. Young plants are needed for them to feed on and tall, older heather to nest and shelter in. For these reasons small strips of heather on grouse moors have been burned in rotation for many decades to create diverse levels of growth within a pair's territory.

Not only is the habitat important but the weather too has a great influence on breeding success. Late frosts freeze eggs in the nest and cold and wet kills newly-hatched chicks. Even mild winters

The red grouse is an indigenous species, unique to Britain.

work against the grouse, for parasites such as ticks, which they share with sheep, thrive in warmer conditions. Another parasite that seriously affects the health of grouse, old and young, is a gut worm called *strongylosis*. Because the birds are completely wild, it is very difficult to treat them with drugs. However supplementary grit that is put out on the moor, which they need to help digest the fibrous heather more efficiently, is sometimes medicated with a wormer.

Gamekeepers are employed to manage the moors by caring for the habitat and maintaining tracks and the butts (hides) in which the shooters stand when grouse are driven over them. Another important aspect of a grouse-keeper's work is the control of predators such as foxes, stoats and crows. His beat may cover several thousand acres and he needs to be very familiar with the ground and aware of what is happening to his birds throughout the year. Grouse shooting is a major source of income on these moors for there is nothing else besides the sheep.

While this intensive management is carried out for the sake of red grouse, many other species benefit. A recent survey showed that 121 different bird species were recorded on areas managed for grouse shooting. Compared with equivalent unkeepered moors, there were four times more golden plover, six times more snipe, five

Above: Two male blackcocks, eager to attract the attention of a female, face up to each other on a lek, the area where they gather to display.

Below left: Grouse are usually driven over a line of shooters who are concealed in 'butts'. These constructions are sometimes dug into the moor or built out of stone, like this well-made example on the North Yorkshire Moors.

times more redshank and three times more dunlin. Curlew, lapwing and blackcock numbers were doubled.

Black grouse or blackcock (*Tetrao tetrix*) – females are called Greyhens – are a rarer member of the grouse family which are only now found in the north of England, where they are also known as 'muircock'. Unlike red grouse which are monogamous, blackcock males in Spring gather in a group on a 'lek' where they try to attract females by 'strutting their stuff'. They were once common on heathlands across the south of England until loss of habitat and over-shooting caused their extinction in that location. On Ashdown Forest in Sussex and the New Forest in Hampshire, a nucleus of stock survived into the 19th century. They lingered until the 1940s on Bodmin Moor and Dartmoor in the West Country. On Exmoor, where they were also known as 'heath poults', the last one was seen in the early 1980s.

Brimstone

Speckled Wood

Small Tortoiseshell

Small White

Comma

Meadow Brown

Common Blue

Small Copper

Gatekeeper

Brown Argus

Red Admiral

Painted Lady

Butterflies in England: 56 Species

There are at least 56 different species of butterflies seen regularly in England but some are in decline. This is mainly due to loss of habitat, for many are very specific as to where they lay their eggs. After about two weeks, butterfly eggs hatch into caterpillars which feed voraciously on the appropriate food plant before maturing into a chrysalis. Most over-winter at this stage before emerging the following year as fully developed adults.

The first butterflies to appear in Spring are normally Brimstones. Orange-tips follow soon after, along with Peacocks. After that many others can be seen throughout the summer. Some butterflies are large such as the beautiful swallowtail now found only on the Norfolk Broads where their caterpillars feed on milk parsley. Caterpillars of the more familiar tortoiseshells, peacocks, painted ladies and red admirals all feed primarily on stinging nettles. Many other species feed on grasses but some are much more selective. Brimstones feed on buckthorn and the Duke of Burgundy fritillary on cowslip and primrose plants.

Small coppers usually choose docks or sorrel and the holly blue, as its name suggests, feeds on the flower buds of holly and also ivy. Elm trees play host to caterpillars of the white-lettered hairstreak the population of which must have been affected by the loss of trees through Dutch elm disease. Oak leaves provide food for purple hairstreak caterpillars and the silver-washed fritillary lays her eggs two or three feet (1m) above the ground on the trunk of an oak tree although the caterpillars, when they hatch, climb down to the ground and find violets to feed on. Even more remarkable are large blues which start life on plants of wild thyme; the caterpillars are then carried away by red ants to their underground chambers where the butterfly larvae eat the young ant larvae, only emerging as a butterfly the following Spring.

Not many insects survive an English winter in adult form but mostly as eggs, grubs or chrysalis. Butterflies are no exception although a few such as brimstone, peacock and tortoiseshell will hide away in buildings. A spell of warm sunshine in January may wake them with fatal consequences. Incredibly, many species migrate here from the Mediterranean. Not only do these delicate insects have to survive the vagaries of an English summer but also the long journey to get here. Monarchs, which regularly migrate 3,000 miles from South America to Canada, have even been recorded here in England.

Butterflies generally fly only during the daytime. Most moths, on the other hand, fly at night. There are around 2,500 species of moths in Britain, many of whom also migrate.

Conservation of Moorland & Heath

Moorland once covered most of the uplands of England but has decreased dramatically since the 1950s when much was lost to farming and forestry. Lowland heaths were formed when Stone Age man began clearing the woods and, in sandy areas, heather grew. Only 10% of lowland heath now remains of what there was a century ago but this loss is slowly being redressed.

Bogs have formed in places where drainage is poor. There are several hundred varieties of mosses as well as other specialist plants to be found in these wet places but it is usually sphagnum moss which dominates.

The soil on moorland is very shallow and lacking in plant nutrients. Where it is covered in grass it is known as 'whitemoor' or more commonly 'white-ground' and generally supports very little in the way of wildlife or livestock. Heather moorland is sometimes described as 'blackmoor' and if it is well managed it provides not only grazing but also a haven for wildlife. Three-quarters of the world's remaining heather moorland is found in Britain. Wild as they seem, these moors are not actually a natural environment and very careful management is needed to preserve them.

Heather will only grow on peat or acid soils and there are three varieties to be found in England of which ling (*Calluna vulgaris*) is by far the most common. Cross-leaved heather grows in wetter places and bell heather prefers well-drained slopes with only a thin layer of peat. Restoration of heather that has been lost can be carried

Below: This little piece of lowland heath has been preserved at Roydon Common in Norfolk.

out by reseeding. This is done by either sowing seed directly into prepared ground or by spreading cut heather over it in October or November so that the seeds can naturally fall out. Heather seed is collected by either vacuuming it up or mechanically collecting the pods.

Between 1945 and 1985, 200,000 acres (81,000ha) of heather moorland was lost but 80% of that has now been restored through regeneration programmes of reseeding.

The conservation of established heather requires a fine balance. It is partly managed by controlled grazing but more importantly by burning, known as 'muirburn' or on Exmoor as 'swaling'. Small patches are burned in rotation every 7-10 years to produce a succession of young heather, forming a patchwork of plants at differing stages of growth. This in turn not only provides grazing for sheep but more importantly a habitat in which wild Red grouse can thrive, for grouse shooting in the north is a major source of income from this otherwise unproductive land.

Burning in England can only be carried out when conditions are right, between 1st October and 15th April in the uplands or from 1st November to 31st March on lower ground. The heather needs to

Above: The golden plover, a species which benefits from conservation work on the heather moorlands.

Above left: Fire is an important tool in the management of heather.

be sufficiently dry to burn properly but the underlying peat must be wet so that it doesn't catch alight. Wind speed and direction have to be taken into consideration and if there aren't any natural grass fire breaks, some need to be cut. The flames are controlled manually by using 'beaters' and in expert hands heather fires very rarely get out of control. Moor grassland also benefits from periodic burning.

Country Shows

Charolais cattle are judged at the Norfolk County Show which is held each year near Norwich.

From Spring until autumn, country shows are held across England. Some such as the Royal Show and the CLA Game Fair are huge, each attracting 130,000 visitors while others are little more than village affairs. It is an opportunity for country folk to show off their animals and catch up with the latest developments in equipment and management. But most of all, whatever size the show, it is a social event and in all probability just as much time is spent talking as it is looking!

County shows often extend to two or three days and are based on agriculture. Originally they were held at different venues around the county but as their popularity grew and people became more mobile, some permanent show grounds were built with excellent

facilities. They also host other events throughout the year such as gardening and antique fairs. The largest country show is the CLA Game Fair which originally began life as a show for those who participated in field sports. However, it soon expanded to include just about every aspect of country life while still maintaining an emphasis on fishing and shooting. One thousand exhibitors cater for every conceivable rural interest and hundreds of competitors take part in clay shooting, fishing and gundog events. The Game Fair takes place for three days over the last weekend in July and is unique in being the biggest countryside show with no permanent venue. The required site needs a large area of relatively level grassland with lakes or a wide river for the fishing and gundog demonstrations and

Above: Local fox hounds parade in the main ring.

Below: Displays and flying demonstrations of birds of prey like this gyr-cross-saker can be seen at many country shows.

competitions, plus adequate parking for thousands of cars. Because of these prerequisites, Game Fairs are held in the beautiful grounds surrounding large country houses such as Broadlands in the south of England and Harewood House in the north.

At the other end of the spectrum are countless little events held across the country which are a microcosm of local rural life. In the north of England it seems that every dale holds a show where sheep and hounds predominate. Local shepherds bring along their sheep to compete with their neighbours or enter their dogs in trials. Hunting is a way of life for many and these shows also provide a chance to show off their hounds. Traditional sports such as Cumbrian wrestling, Fell running, hound trailing and horn blowing add more competition to the day. The roots of these shows go back to the days before motor cars when life rarely extended farther than the dale, and still they are an opportunity for isolated rural communities with common interests to meet together. For those unfamiliar with rural life these little shows may seem insignificant but they are like pages in a history book recording how true country people are still living and working at the beginning of the 21st century.

Derbyshire Well Dressing

The custom of well dressing in England has its home in the Derbyshire Peak District where it has been the tradition for centuries to give thanks for the water they provide by decorating the wells in many of the villages. It's thought the tradition dates back to pagan times, compounded by the fact that a 'Well Queen', once a symbol of fertility, is sometimes elected.

Legend has it that the purity of water from the wells in Tissington saved villagers from destruction during the Black Death plague that struck the surrounding area in 1349. In gratitude, people made offerings of flowers and, ever since, the ritual has continued. This even extended to tap dressing in Wirkworth which celebrated the arrival of piped water in 1827!

Originally, wells were bedecked with garlands in a ceremony known as 'well flowering' but in the 19th century, more elaborate decorations were used. The custom all-but died out in the 1950s but since then has been revived. About 60 towns and villages in the Peak District now join in with the celebrations and some have several carefully preserved wells which are dressed for a week each year.

From the beginning of May through to early September, villages across Derbyshire celebrate the custom. An inauguration ceremony, sometimes including a blessing, is held to mark the occasion and the theme is generally pastoral or depicts famous local people or events. Flower petals, seeds, berries, moss, alder cones, bark, wool, twigs and slate are painstakingly fixed into a clay base within a wooden frame to create a detailed picture. Only natural materials can be used. Preparation is a major social event in each village as locals spend many hours slowly piecing pictures together. Although well dressing is not competitive, much pride and satisfaction is felt when the results of all the hard work go on public view.

Every summer at Ashford-in-the-Water, Derbyshire, the six village wells are decorated with floral pictures as a thanksgiving for the purity of their water.

SEPTEMBER

The Norfolk Broads consist of more than 40 freshwater lakes in east Norfolk and Suffolk, the largest of which is the 350 acre (140 hectare) Hickling Broad. They are linked by 125 miles (200kms) of navigable waterways and they discharge into Breydon Water, a three and a half mile (6km) long tidal estuary which flows into the North Sea at Great Yarmouth. The Broads complex was created out of fenland by peat digging in medieval times and most of the water is pumped from surrounding rivers, dykes and streams although some also comes from springs. Once the Broads were full of plant life but in many places they became polluted in the 1960s. Conservationists are working to restore the water quality but this is difficult due to the popularity of leisure craft which can be hired on an hourly, daily or weekly basis. Speed limits are imposed to reduce erosion of the banks. With one million holidaymakers and one million day trippers now visiting the Broads annually, pollution and congestion continue to be a challenge. Windmills dot the flat landscape, many of which have been converted into houses.

Above: The Suffolk church at Dedham is traditionally decorated for Harvest Festival.

Opposite: The little country church at Marham in Norfolk holds a flower festival to coincide with its Harvest Festival celebrations.

Harvest Festival

September 29th is Michaelmas, the old English name for the feast day of St Michael and All Angels. Traditionally, it is also the end of the farming year, a time when farms change ownership or tenancies. It is the time when most crops should have been harvested and harvest festivals are held in village churches across England.

Many villages still celebrate the fact that 'all is safely gathered in' with a harvest supper, just as farm workers have done for centuries. In the Middle Ages 'Harvest Home' was celebrated in the farmer's house. A symbolic corn dolly of plaited straw would be made from the last sheaf of corn and carried aloft to the celebrations. It would be kept in the farmhouse until the next harvest supper.

The religious festival as we know it today was introduced by a Cornish vicar in the middle of the nineteenth century and is yet another pagan custom adopted by the Christian church.

It is only since the 1960s that the vital necessity of producing home-grown food has become less important. It used to be a great relief for our forefathers to know the toils of Spring and summer had ensured that barns were full of winter fodder for livestock, barley to feed them, seed to sow in the coming Spring and wheat to feed themselves.

Out in the countryside every autumn, women would have not only helped with the harvest but also been busy gathering and preserving fruits from the hedgerows and orchards. Jams, pickles and chutneys would be lined up on the pantry shelves.

It was indeed a time to go to church and thank God for providing enough food to be harvested and stored until the following summer, when fresh food once again became available. Progress has changed all that. Planes and fast ships transport produce from the four corners of the world, so most foresee no reason why we should ever run short of food. In England it is no longer such a struggle

to make hay or harvest corn during bad weather. Huge modern machines can devour several acres of crops when there's a fine day. The urgency has gone and with it, the appreciation. Fewer people work on the land, but those who still do have not forgotten and what was probably once the most important religious event in the agri-cultural calendar continues to be celebrated each year. Produce from the harvest festival was distributed among the poor of the parish and today is often given away to local charities. Churches are still symbolically decorated with corn, vegetables and fruit and many now incorporate a flower festival with their display.

Bringing in the Potato Crop

The humble spud was cultivated 5,000 years ago in Peru and brought to England from South America by explorers in the late 16th century. Sir Walter Raleigh is sometimes credited with its introduction, but it was more than a century before it became a staple part of the English diet. Surprisingly, potatoes didn't reach North America until 1719 when they were taken there by Irish immigrants. The nickname 'spud' originates from a medieval word for a dagger or short knife which was then applied to the narrow spade used for digging the soil. By about 1850 it was also being used to describe the potato tuber itself which needed to be planted in holes in the ground.

Many varieties of potato have been developed over the centuries for their size and disease-resistance. Some are waxy in texture and hold together better when cooked, while others are softer and starchy. In recent years, specific varieties have been developed for making crisps, chips and mashed potato. Although the flesh of a potato is white or cream-coloured, the skin colour varies. Some popular ones such as 'Desiree' have red skins, 'King Edwards' are white with red patches and the 'Estima' is all white. As consumers become more discerning, flavour has become an increasingly important factor.

In Spring, potatoes are planted singly, deep in the ground beneath ridges of soil; and from each one, several more develop. They must be kept covered by earth for they turn green when exposed to daylight and become inedible. The tubers also push up luxuriant leaves through the soil which have pretty white or mauve flowers but the leaves cannot be eaten as the stems, foliage and cherry-sized berries which develop all contain a poisonous alkaloid. If the tops

Harvesting the main potato crop begins in September.

are still green when it's time to harvest the potatoes, they are usually sprayed to kill the growth.

Early crops fetch premium prices and are most likely to be grown in milder southern counties of England such as Cornwall. Sometimes they are covered in plastic to hasten growth and protect them from frosts but generally, English new potatoes don't become widely available until late May. Harvesting of the main crop doesn't begin until September. Before farming became fully mechanised, potatoes were spun out of the ground with a horse-drawn implement and picked up by hand, often by women and children. They would then be stored in a heap and protected against frost with a covering of straw and earth. This was known as a 'clamp'.

Rape stubbles are ripped up in these last days of summer so that the next crop can be planted.

Modern methods now enable potatoes to be mechanically dug and loaded straight into trailers. They can be kept in prime condition throughout the winter in temperature and humidity-controlled sheds. Potatoes are susceptible to many diseases, viruses and pests, all of which are aggravated by adverse weather conditions. Trials are taking place with genetically modified potatoes that are resistant to blight, a very common disease which causes discolouration and rotting of the tubers.

147

Outdoor Pigs

Pigs are kept outdoors in many areas of England where the ground doesn't get too waterlogged in winter. Labour and feed costs are higher for outdoor pigs than for those kept intensively, but housing costs are lower as no specialist buildings are required. The concept of animals being kept out of doors is also more satisfying to the customer. Producers marketing their pigs under quality-assured schemes have to abide by stringent regulations laid down for welfare and management, with regular veterinary inspections taking place. The 'Little Red Tractor' is an easily-recognised symbol providing assurance that meat is home-produced to certain standards.

Outdoor pigs are generally kept in small groups in fields which have been divided into paddocks with low electric fences. Shelters are provided not only for protection against rain and snow but also against the sun, for pigs are very susceptible to sunburn. Large flat water troughs are also a feature, allowing pigs to bathe or wallow in the surrounding muddy area. This coating of mud helps protect them from sunburn.

Most commercial sows are white hybrids which are long in the body and have been specially bred for their leanness. A young sow is known as a 'gilt' and she is first mated when she is about eight months old. After that she will be expected to produce a litter of ten or more piglets every five to six months.

Sows are run with a boar for a few weeks before being moved into another paddock. Just before giving birth they are moved again to a maternity section furnished with individual huts. Here after a pregnancy lasting 17 weeks, each sow will make herself a nest from the straw provided and give birth to (farrow) as many as 14 piglets. A low barrier is put in front of each hut to prevent the little pigs

A hybrid outdoor pig, bred especially for its leanness, looking pink and perky.

148

Above: Organically-raised pigs enjoying an outdoor life.

Right: Pigs love wallowing in mud, and are encouraged to do so, as it protects them from sunburn.

from wandering off but by the time they are three weeks old they are big enough to scramble over it.

They are weaned at about four weeks and kept in groups in nursery huts with open runs until they are about three months old, by which time they should weigh approximately 88lbs (40kgs). The young pigs are then housed indoors for a further 10-12 weeks until they are ready for slaughter at about 200lbs (98kgs).

There are about four million pigs in Britain, of which nearly a quarter are kept outdoors.

Growing hops the old-fashioned way in a 'hop garden'.

Small Breweries Make a Come-back

Kent was once renowned for its 'hop gardens' and until the early 1950s families moved there from London for a few weeks in late summer to pick them. Although beer production may appear to be a fairly simple process, it is in fact a very complex one. Beer continues to be a popular drink in England and through the initiative of CAMRA (The Campaign for Real Ale) the recent expansion of micro-breweries has ensured that traditional methods of brewing are preserved. It is the skills of these individual brewers which have resulted in the wide choice of cask brews now available.

The three principal ingredients of beer are barley, hops and yeast although other grains besides barley may also be used. The early Egyptians first discovered the art of brewing beer, and hops have been used for more than 2,500 years. Hops (*Humulus lupulus*) grew wild in England long before they were first cultivated for beer-production early in the 16th century. Only the flowers of female plants develop into the actual hops which are pale green leafy cones covered in resinous glands.

Not so very long ago these vigorous climbers were trained up poles 14ft high with wire stretched between. Men on stilts would secure the plants as they grew, and in late summer, when the hops were ripe, the whole plant would be cut down. The hops were then taken to be dried in the distinctive local 'oast houses'. Now hops are trained along low fences where they can be harvested by a machine straddling the row. They are also grown in areas around Warwickshire, Shropshire and Suffolk.

To begin the beer-making process, barley is first 'malted' by soaking in water. It is then allowed to germinate before being roasted to halt the growth. Starch in cereals doesn't ferment but this process converts the starch to fermentable sugar. The barley is then ground before hot water is added to produce a sugary infusion known as 'wort'. Dried hops, which add bitterness, along with spices, herbs or other flavours are added to give the brew a distinctive flavour. Some-

ve: Oast houses in Kent once dried hops but are now residential conversions.

w: A choice of beers from the Iceni micro brewery at Ickburgh in Norfolk.

times additional sugar is included at this stage to raise the final alcohol level. The wort is cooled, yeast added and it is left to ferment for two or more days, depending on the type of beer. It is then allowed to settle before being bottled or put into metal barrels.

'Keg' beer, mass produced by the large breweries, only goes through a primary fermentation process; the fizz is added artificially when it is served. 'Cask' beer, on the other hand, has the yeast left in it, producing a beer with only natural gases.

Even after bottling, the process of fermentation continues and will slightly alter the flavour depending on how long the beer is kept. The length of time barley is roasted or steeped, the choice and amount of herbs, spices and hops added and the lengths of time beer is stored all influence the taste.

There are several basic types of English beer. Bitter is heavily hopped, mild ale is lightly hopped and low in alcohol. Stout is a dark beer made from heavily roasted malts, sometimes sweet with low alcohol content, but more often stout is dry and bitter with a high alcohol level.

Ale and beer are produced in different ways. Beer (and lager) is made with bottom-fermenting yeasts at a low temperature (5-9°C) and is stored at 0°C for 3-12 weeks before use. Beer should be served at room temperature and lager should be served cold. Ale is made with yeast that floats on top of the wort which is fermented quickly at a higher temp (15-25°C) and can be served soon after this process is complete.

Each product has a specific storage period before being canned, bottled, kegged or kept in unpressurised casks. With national and regional breweries plus more than 500 micro-breweries in the UK, the choice is infinite and there are ample opportunities to sample the range at beer festivals held across the country.

The Otter and the Mink

The otter (*Lutra lutra*) conservation story is one of success. Otters have lived in Britain for more than 10,000 years but a combination of events caused a dramatic decline in numbers during the 1960s and nearly wiped them out. The waterways that otters were living on became polluted through increased use of chemicals.

Pesticides and herbicides entered the food chain, resulting in slow poisoning. The otter population was also affected by other pollutants such as silage effluent and nitrates which leached from the soil. Harsh winters, human activities and habitat destruction also played their part in the otter's decline. Although hunting was also blamed, it was in fact the hunters who conserved otters in many places and they who first became aware of the problem and not only publicised the fact but voluntarily stopped hunting. Otters were given full protection soon after.

Gradually, conservation efforts have paid off. By 1995 23% of rivers once again had otters and in 2005 this figure had risen to 36% with the work still continuing. A release programme was spearheaded by the Otter Trust, a registered charity, and it wasn't long before those released were spreading to new territories and even breeding with the few remaining wild otters.

Otters are shy and mainly nocturnal so are rarely seen. The most obvious indication of their presence in an area is from the number of road casualties, for otters travel long distances across land, inevitably having to cross roads in the process.

Otters belong to the same family as stoats and weasels. The

Above: 36% of English rivers now have an otter population.

Below: The mink, a relatively new species in England, can easily be mistaken for a young otter.

The re-introduction of the otter has been a conservation success.

males are called 'dogs' and weigh up to 25lbs (12kgs) and females are called 'bitches'. The dens they live in are known as 'holts'. Two or three young cubs are usually born in Spring but can arrive at any time of the year and they stay with their mother for about a year. Father does not get involved with cub-rearing for long.

Otters eat mostly fish and are sometimes unwanted visitors to fisheries. One of their favourite prey is eels. These aquatic animals are very agile under water, their progress revealed by a trail of bubbles rising to the surface. They are seldom found around the English coast. Otters have an acute sense of smell and mark their large territories with faeces often deposited on a tuft of grass, a stone or under a bridge. These droppings have a sweet, musky smell and are known as 'spraints'.

Mink (*Mustela vison*), the otter's North American cousins who have invaded England's rivers, are often mistaken for young otters as they are very similar in appearance.

Otters are secretive animals, for the most part steering clear of people. When alarmed they dive, a trail of bubbles betraying their position under water.

Saving the English Partridge

In September, you might be lucky enough to spot a family band of Grey or English partridge (*Perdix perdix*) on an uncultivated stubble field. They are indigenous to Britain but are suffering a serious decline. The Game Conservancy Trust has for many years been researching the reasons and trying to find solutions to the crisis. At the root of the problem are modern farming methods which not only destroy the habitat but also leave little grain or seed for partridges to feed on. Agricultural herbicides and pesticides also destroy the majority of the much-needed insects, grubs and plants they live on, which the newly-hatched chicks particularly need to survive their first few weeks.

Grey Partridges are not easy to rear in captivity so although they are highly-valued as game birds, the wild population is not generally supplemented. Partridges are naturally birds of arable farmland and hedgerows. In some areas of England, especially the south-west, Greys have become a rarity. They are now most likely to be found in East Anglia, on chalk downland and the fringes of moorland.

Many of the estates where they are still found have shooting interests and they go to great lengths to preserve and increase what stock they already have. Measures include planting special crops, leaving grassy banks across the middle of fields where insects can thrive and controlling predators such as crows, stoats and foxes which destroy nests and kill young birds.

Grey partridges choose a mate in winter and stay together as a pair for most of the year. Their creaking call has been likened to the sound of a rusty gate hinge. Nests are well hidden in vegetation, often close to a hedge. More than 20 eggs may be laid and of all the birds in Britain, the Grey partridge lays most eggs. Each time the hen bird leaves her nest she carefully covers the eggs with grass or leaves. While she is incubating them, the

Grey Partridges – breeding pairs are touchingly loyal and devoted to each other for most of the year.

Right: French Partridges, also known as Red-legged Partridges, are bred on sporting estates and are now more commonly seen in the English countryside than the Grey Partridges.

Above: Newly-hatched Grey Partridge chicks are little bigger than bumble bees.

cock sits close by and will try to defend her from anything that gets too close. As the chicks begin to hatch he stays near to the hen and calls them to him so they can find warmth beneath his body. Peak hatching time is usually in the third week of June coinciding with Royal Ascot race week. Weather at that time is critical for the tiny bumblebee-sized chicks cannot survive if it is wet and cold. Sadly, although Grey partridge are the most devoted of parents, with such a large brood to care for, many die. They remain in a family group, known as a 'covey', until the winter.

Although similar in appearance, the Red-legged partridge (*Alectoris rufa*), also called the French partridge, is genetically different to the Grey. Charles II has been credited with importing birds from the Mediterranean in 1673 to stock his royal hunting parks at Richmond and Windsor. Others believe they didn't arrive until a century later but since then they have gradually established themselves across England. However, they are not as hardy as Greys and thrive best on lighter land which is not too exposed.

Red-legs are quite placid by nature and, during the last 50 years, they have increasingly been reared in captivity and released for shooting. They are considered to be inferior as sporting game birds because they are less inclined to fly than Greys, nor do Red-legs have such a high culinary reputation. In the wild Red-legs are not such loyal or conscientious parents as our native partridges and the hen is often left to rear her brood on her own.

Wasps Solitary and Social

Beware the wasp in September, irritably drunk on fermented fallen fruit in an orchard!

There are several different species of wasp leading diverse lifestyles: some are 'solitary' and some are 'sociable' wasps. The one with which we are most familiar in England, mostly through unpleasant experiences, is the Common wasp (*Vespa vulgaris*) which can sting continuously, unlike a bee which dies after having stung only once. A further difference between bees and wasps is that wasps do not store food for the winter. All wasps die except the mated queen which hides away in sheds or under tree bark.

In Spring she seeks out a place to nest: it may be in a roof cavity, under the eaves, or quite often a hole in the ground. There she makes a rudimentary nest in which she lays several eggs which develop into larvae. As female workers hatch, they extend the nest by collecting rotten wood from trees or boards etc which they mix with saliva to produce a grey paper-like substance. The larvae are carnivorous and workers gather animal matter and insects with which to feed them. In return they feed on the sweet saliva which the grubs produce.

Breeding continues, with a few males developing in late summer to mate with a new generation of queens. The original queen ceases to lay and it is at this time that adult Common wasps become a nuisance as deprived of saliva from the grubs they go

Above: A 'Robin's Pin Cushion' develops on the wild dog rose after a gall wasp has laid its egg on one of the leaf buds.

156

in search of nectar and sweet fruits. The European wasp, which is appearing each year in greater numbers, is very similar and noted for its bad temper. Tree wasps (*Dolichovespula sylvestris*) are also social and build their nests hanging from the branch of a bush. Another species known as Cuckoo wasps are parasitic and lay their eggs in the nests of other wasps.

There are many solitary wasps such as the Spider-eating wasp and the Mason wasp which tunnels into walls and makes tiny nests. The female wasp places a captured caterpillar within each chamber for the larva to feed on when it hatches.

Gall wasps are small ant-like insects which are also solitary but they lay their eggs on plants. When the egg hatches, an abnormal swelling or gall develops around the larva, on which it feeds. The most obvious galls are those of the Bedeguar gall wasp (*Diplolepis rosae*) that develop from leaf buds into 'robin's pin cushions' on wild dog rose. Several different gall wasps lay their eggs on oak trees which react to form a protective gall full of soft pulp on which the developing grub feeds.

One species of wasp causes the 'spangles' that can be found on the underside of oak leaves, another attacks acorns which results in them becoming deformed. The Oak apple gall wasp lays several eggs under a bud. In early stages of development the growth is similar in colour to an apple but later becomes brown and spongy. Brown marble-sized balls attached to a small oak branch have been home to Marble gall wasps and closer inspection will reveal a small hole in each from which the wasp has bored out.

Because a Hornet (*Vespa crabro*) is twice the size of a wasp, people tend to be more scared of them but generally they are quite placid and only attack when provoked. They have similar habits to the Common wasp but live in smaller colonies and are found predominately in the south of England.

Below left: Common wasps sometimes take over a nesting box put up for birds – like this blue-tit box.

Below centre: Wood wasps usually build their nests around the branches of a bush.

Below right: Sap on the trunk of an ash tree is food for a hornet.

Fenland Conservation

Much of East Anglia used to be fenland. Today, a large area spanning parts of west Norfolk, Cambridgeshire and Lincolnshire is still known as the Fens although it bears little resemblance to what it once was. The Romans were aware of the richness of the fertile soil across this low-lying area but each winter local rivers overflowed, foiling their attempts to reclaim it.

It wasn't until 1632 that Dutchman Cornelius Vermuyden devised a successful plan to drain the fens. He straightened rivers, built banks and dug an artificial 'cut' (canal) known as the Bedford river between Earith and Denver which was 21 miles (34km) long and 70ft (21m) wide.

Work was interrupted by the Civil War but afterwards another artificial channel was constructed now known as the New Bedford river. Further drainage was achieved with a network of smaller drains and dykes (ditches) with water pumped from these into the rivers, at first by windmills, from 1820 onwards by steam engines and then by electric motors.

The gradual drying out of this black peaty soil created problems of its own for it was, and still is, very unstable. Many early brick buildings gradually cracked and sunk, some ending up leaning at an angle, while others required additional steps building up to the door, as the land around them shrunk.

Continued cultivation of the fens is still causing damage for in Spring when the ground is bare and a strong drying wind sweeps unhindered across the flat land, it carries the soil away in dust storms. Erosion over the years has lowered the soil in some places by as much as 12ft (3.5m) and left it below sea level. Many river levels are higher than the surrounding land and have to be contained within substantial banks. Uneven fen roads are notoriously dangerous and some run alongside rivers and dykes with no fence or bank to separate them.

Visitors to the fens might spot small islands of slightly raised ground where isolated communities once lived amidst the swampy wetlands, living off the fenland plants, fish and wildfowl. They walked on stilts, dug peat for fuel and thatched their huts with sedge. Many areas are still known as 'poor fens' which gave local villagers the rights to collect peat and cut sedge. The inhabitants fiercely resented the Dutch drainage engineers who called these hostile people 'Fen Tigers'.

In 673AD a Saxon princess by the name of St Ethelreda founded a religious community on the Isle of Ely. Later in 1081 this became the site for Ely cathedral which rises majestically above the surrounding fenland.

Fragmented pockets of ancient, fragile fens can still be found and conservationists are working hard to preserve them. Wicken Fen in Cambridgeshire is the most substantial area remaining. Owned by the National Trust it extends to 600 acres (240h) and offers access via nature trails and board walks. It became Britain's first designated nature reserve in 1899.

It wasn't until 1982 that remains of a one-kilometre wooden barrier built in 1,350BC was discovered at Flag Fen near Peterborough. Bronze Age artefacts were also found preserved in the surrounding water-logged peat. A museum and reconstruction there show how Bronze Age people lived in the Fens.

Recently Sutton Fen in the Norfolk Broads became the RSPB's 200th reserve. Several other small pockets of fen are being preserved by local wildlife trusts and other organisations with the help of volunteers.

These habitats support a unique diversity of flora and fauna, some of which are very rare such as the Raft spider (*Dolomedes plantarius*) and Swallowtail butterfly (*Papilio machaon*).

Opposite: Classic fenland at Wicken Fen, Cambridgeshire.

Right: The Fen Raft Spider, which hunts its prey in water, can be found at Redgrave and Lopham Fen, habitats managed by the Suffolk Wildlife Trust.

Top: The rare Swallow Tail butterfly is now confined to the Norfolk Broads where it can be seen earlier in the summer.

Above: Southern Hawker dragonflies can often be seen patrolling the fen waterways.

The Great English Pub

One of the delights of travelling through the English countryside is to see the assortment of public houses along the way. Pub signs provide an illustrated guide to the history of England, depicting sports, trades, royalty, local landowners, religious influences and even rustic humour.

The Romans brought pub signs to England, their trading sign of a bush denoting the sale of alcohol. In the early Middle Ages, ale house keepers put up illustrated signs for the illiterate majority. Religious houses opened hostelries for pilgrims in the 12th century in which an anchor denoted the Christian faith. Shortly afterwards knights on their way to the Crusades made use of inns which inspired pub names such as the *Saracen's Head* and Nottingham's ancient *Ye Olde Trip To Jerusalem*.

A few existing inns have had their timber work carbon dated to the tenth century and many date back at least 600 years. *The Bingley Arms* at Bardsey in West Yorkshire claims to be one of the oldest, parts of which date back to 905.

Inns were originally staging posts on major routes where travellers and their horses could find accommodation and food. Situated in the north of the Yorkshire Dales the isolated *Tan Hill Inn* is the highest pub in England at 1,732ft (531m) above sea level. In 1830 *The Beer House Act* allowed a much larger number of drinking places to open, many of which later became public houses.

Until well into the 1900s it was a sanctum for men only. Some pubs served only beer for rural labourers to quench their thirst after a day's hard work, perhaps also playing shove-ha'penny, darts, cards, skittles or dominoes. But the biggest change to the village pub came when drink-driving laws were introduced in the 1970s. To protect their livelihoods, pub landlords turned to serving food as well as alcohol and country pubs have now become places that provide meals and a welcome for all the family. Some have gained a reputation for serving high quality food.

Above: The Bell at Kersey, Suffolk. *Far Left*: Sign at the Royal Oak, Barcombe, Sussex. *Left*: White Hart at South Harting in West Sussex.

OCTOBER

The leaves of deciduous trees contain green, sugar-producing chlorophyll; and carotene, an orange pigment that protects against ultra-violet rays. As days shorten, trees begin to shut down and the green of the chlorophyll fades, allowing carotene to show through. In sunlight, sugars in the leaves form the most wonderful autumn shades of yellow, gold, orange and red. A hard frost hastens the process but in recent years, warmer temperatures have gradually nudged this breathtaking autumn spectacle from late October into November. Larch is one of the most beautiful conifers with its delicate branches and it is the only one to shed its needles in winter. Its identity is obscured amid the greens of summer but revealed again when autumn arrives, as each needle turns a pale shade of yellow. The above scene is Tarn Hows in the Lake District.

Halloween's Pagan Roots

Halloween is traditionally celebrated on 31st October but its roots are in an old Celtic autumn festival. It was once the Druid festival of Samhain (pronounced 'sow inn') on the eve of the Pagan New Year, celebrating the end of harvesting crops and a time when livestock were slaughtered and preserved for winter. It heralded the start of the period of darkness and cold.

Samhain was also thought to be the supernatural time when barriers between the earthly and the spirit world were at their weakest, and restless spirits would return from the dead. Bonfires were lit and burning torches carried round villages to scare away the evil spirits. It is yet another example of how paganism and Christianity have merged together. All Hallows Eve (Hallowe'en) is the evening before All Hallows (or All Saints) Day. The following day is All Souls Day when everyone who has died is remembered. The Christian church does not celebrate with fire as the pagans did but it believes that Jesus cast light on the world, defeating all fears of darkness, and it frequently uses candles symbolically.

Further connections with the festival of Samhain extended into November but have been condensed into Hallowe'en as we know it.

A grand October display of pumpkins grown by Ralph Upton from Slindon in West Sussex.

November 4th was once 'mischief day' when children would play practical jokes. They dressed in disguise so that ghouls wouldn't be able to recognise them.

Pumpkins have replaced the potatoes, beet, swedes and turnips which were once carved into Jack-o-Lanterns. After being hollowed out and sculpted with a spooky face, a candle is lit inside and the lantern put outside the door. The candle flame, symbolic of the fires and burning torches, is intended to frighten away witches and ghosts. November 5th with its bonfires and noise was probably originally associated with scaring away evil spirits at this time of year.

About one million pumpkins are now bought each October, 99% of which are used to make lanterns. The flesh can be used to make pies, jams and chutneys, and increasing interest is being taken in its culinary values.

Fields of pumpkins become more obvious in autumn as the fruits swell and turn yellow and orange. The largest producer in England farms near Spalding in Lincolnshire. Competition across England today is fierce to grow the largest pumpkin. In 2006 a new UK record pumpkin weighing 1,124 lbs (511 kg) was grown in Hampshire.

The legendary Mr Ralph Upton from Slindon in West Sussex has been growing pumpkins, gourds and squashes for more than 50 years. 15,000 are harvested annually from 55 varieties which have been cultivated in a four acre walled garden. His large orange 'sunset' pumpkin measures up to three feet (one metre) across and weighs nearly 200lbs (90kg) but many others are much smaller as are the gourds and squashes which come in many different sizes, shapes and colours.

Above: Carving out pumpkins for Halloween.

Below: Pumpkins, gourds and squashes come in many shapes, sizes and colours.

Markets' Busiest Time of Year

The centre of nearly every English country town used to have a live-stock market but, being prime development sites, few are now left. Some had closure forced upon them as a result of restrictions during the Foot and Mouth Disease outbreak in 2001. Many markets have been re-built on more practical sites on the outskirts of town and now diversify by holding other types of auctions.

Market towns also had small abattoirs supplying local butchers with carcases which were then prepared into joints, chops, mince and sausages. It was commonplace to see a quarter of a bullock, half a pig or a whole lamb hung up in the shop.

However, welfare regulations affected the transit and sale of livestock, hygiene regulations forced many small abattoirs to close and supermarkets have displaced some local butchers.

For the last 25 years or so, many suppliers of pigs, cattle and lambs have begun to sell their animals, under contract, direct to supermarkets and processors which use their own abattoirs. Fewer animals destined for the plate are now sold through auction markets but there is still a lively trade for stores (animals for fattening) and breeding stock, with special sales being scheduled regularly.

In early autumn, when grass stops growing, many young cattle and lambs not big enough to kill are sold through markets as 'stores'. These are bought by other farmers who have grazing still available or who can overwinter them in barns while they grow bigger. It is in the grassland regions of England, mainly in the north and west where the farms are mostly small, that local livestock markets still flourish.

Herdwick store lambs enter the ring at Cockermouth Market, Cumbria. This breed is native to Cumbria and the young are always dark-coloured.

Autumn is a busy time of year when thousands of lambs which grazed the moors and Fells all summer are weaned and go under the auctioneer's hammer. Markets have always been a meeting place for folk with a common interest who live in comparative isolation. For many farmers, market day is the one day of the week when work clothes can be discarded and other business, such as getting a haircut, can be done while in town. Incorporated within modern market complexes, there may also be such things as banking facilities and outlets selling farm hygiene products. Most important of all though, at the hub of things, is the market café catering for fresh-air appetites while serving large mugs of tea.

The market still is a place to see old acquaintances, catch up with gossip, perhaps do a deal, ridicule impractical legislation and generally lament the way the agricultural community is treated by the EU and the government.

Top: Herdwick sheep of all ages at Cockermouth Market.

Above: Young cattle are sold at Leyburn Market in the Yorkshire Dales.

Ploughing and Picking

In October it becomes a race against time to get harvest fields ploughed, cultivated and re-sown before the weather becomes too wet and cold. Pre-mechanisation, a man and a pair of horses pulling a single furrow plough would walk 11 miles (18kms) in a day to plough an acre of land. Now great monsters mounted with nine furrow reversible ploughs do it in a fraction of the time. On reaching the end of a strip the plough is flipped over as the tractor turns and returns to plough another nine furrows. On light land a 'press' is often attached to the tractor or plough which breaks and levels the soil at the same time. Acrobatic gulls follow closely as the soil is turned, revealing a veritable feast of worms and grubs.

October is also the month when apples are harvested. They were once an important English crop, used for eating raw, cooking, juice and of course cider-making for which Somerset has long been renowned. Pectin, a natural thickening agent, is also extracted from apples and used to set jellies and jams which are otherwise deficient in pectin. Kent, Somerset and Herefordshire were all once famed for their orchards but cheap imports and other economic factors have resulted in many being grubbed out or standing neglected. In 1974 there were 60,000 acres (25,000 hectares) of orchards in Kent alone, growing cherries, plums, pears and apples for the London markets.

There are hundreds of varieties of apples. Some are thought to have been introduced by the Romans while others arrived in the reign of Henry VIII. Varieties of apples are constantly being improved but even so many old favourites have stood the test of time. The Bramley, still the most popular cooking apple, was first recorded in the early 1800s and delicious Cox's Orange Pippins also date back to the 19th century. Many counties now hold 'apple days'

where old varieties which have been preserved are on display. People are also encouraged to bring along apples from any old trees they have in their gardens to be identified. It's thought there are probably more varieties still undiscovered for many were often very local to a certain area. The old adage 'an apple a day keeps the doctor away' has medical backing and is not just an old wives' tale.

The Brogdale Horticultural Trust near Faversham in Kent is home to the national fruit collection and has 150 acres of orchards growing some 3,639 varieties of British fruit including plums, cherries and pears. Incredibly they have 1,867 different varieties of apples as well as a further 95 varieties of cider apples.

Right: Apple varieties on display at the Apple Day at Stow Bardolph.

Below: There are fewer apple orchards in England than there were 40 years ago.

Heavy Horse Work

It is estimated that in 1910 there were more than a million horses working on farms, most of which were heavy horses used for agricultural work. When mechanisation really took hold in the 1950s cart horses disappeared at an alarming rate.

It wasn't long before the Scottish Clydesdale, the French Percheron, the East Anglian Suffolk and the massive Shires from Middle England were facing extinction. Fortunately there were enough interested people who recognised this threat and set about preserving these magnificent animals. Better still, they ensured that these horses were still able to do the work for which they were originally bred, thus safeguarding the dying skills of the old horseman.

Clydesdales originated in Lanarkshire and are usually black, bay or brown in colour with a lot of white on their face and legs running up to the underbelly. One of their most outstanding qualities is the strength of their legs and particularly the feet. The placid Percherons are black or grey and although they have deep bodies and short legs, they are very active.

The two native English breeds are thought to have developed from war horses which carried Elizabethan knights into battle. Very strong horses were needed to bear the 30 stone (190kgs) burden of a man in shining armour. The Shire is most often seen today pulling wagons and is a favourite of the breweries. It is the largest of the heavy horses and can be of any colour and stand over 18 hands (6ft or 2.72m) high at the shoulders. These gentle giants often have white feet and a blaze on their foreheads; another distinctive feature is their feathered (very hairy) legs below the knee.

The Suffolk is very broad and has short legs with no feathering, to which mud tends to cling. Suffolks are always a shade of chestnut in colour but a white star on the forehead is accepted. The breed is

Roger Clark from Stoke-by-Nayland in Suffolk stlll uses horses to do much of his farmwork.

the oldest in Britain, dating back to the 16th century. The ancestry of every Suffolk horse alive today is said to trace back to 'Crisp's Horse of Ufford' which was born in 1768. During its commercial working life, the Suffolk Punch was very much a breed local to the eastern counties of England but this area was one of the first to become agriculturally mechanised and numbers fell rapidly. In 1966 only nine foals were born. Even now there are only 300 breeding mares with only 30-40 youngsters being registered annually which makes Suffolks rarer than giant pandas.

Each autumn, ploughing matches are held across England, with classes for heavy horses. Each pair is allocated a strip of land to plough, and it is a fantastic sight to watch them doing the work they were bred for, and to see the care and pride their handler takes. The single furrow has to be absolutely straight and the plough carefully adjusted to turn the soil over so any surface debris is buried.

Some owners work their horses in ordinary harness but others display yet another skill in the way they turn their horses out. Many hours beforehand are spent braiding straw in the mane and cleaning leather and brass so that it gleams in the autumn sunshine. Plumes and plaited ribbons reflect the way their ancestors, the medieval warhorses, were adorned with heraldic decorations. There are about 4,000 different designs of horse-brass, many of which incorporate pagan symbols designed to ward off evil spirits and until the early 1800s they were all hand-made.

The horsemen of old knew many ways to get the best out of their animals and it's a great day out to see dedicated enthusiasts retaining their knowledge and practising their skills.

Top: Clydesdales in all their finery at a ploughing match in Suffolk.

Above: The grey Percheron 'Baron' is flanked by Suffolk Punches 'Keepsake' and 'Archie'

Badger Watching

Badgers (*Meles meles*) are very strong. Their short legs, large feet and huge claws are all indications that they are very good at excavating soil. In woodland, on banks and even in the middle of fields, great mounds of earth reveal their presence and well-worn paths lead to and from the holes. Some sites are extensive and known to have been occupied for a very long time.

Badger 'setts' comprise a labyrinth of deep passages, with chambers in which a nest is made from dry vegetation. Badgers are fastidious creatures and regularly change their bedding by reversing down the holes with fresh material held between their front legs and chin. They never foul the ground outside the setts but use latrines.

Females are slightly smaller than males which weigh in the region of 40lbs (18kgs) and are nearly 36 inches (one metre) in length. Badgers are very powerful animals with extremely strong jaws. They are opportunist omnivores but they do not prey on birds and animals in the way a fox does.

Much of their diet consists of worms supplemented with grubs, beetles, bulbs, roots and fruits. They dig out the underground nests of wasps and bumble-bees and also know how to deal with the protective spines of hedgehogs.

Badgers live in family groups and are largely nocturnal.

Badgers live in communal groups and since becoming fully protected in 1992 have steadily increased both in numbers and in their range. Their original stronghold was in the south west of England but they have now taken up residence in places they were previously rarely seen, even in towns.

Badgers can mate at any time of the year but, like roe deer and stoats, implantation of the fertilised eggs is delayed, so the three or four young are not born until February. They are very nocturnal by nature and, apart from road casualties, are rarely seen in daylight. Badgers have thick coats and don't hibernate in winter although activity is curtailed in periods of cold weather. Their hair makes the finest shaving brushes, artists' brushes and in Scotland the traditional sporran.

Badgers are probably the most controversial wild animal in the English countryside. As their numbers increase so does the harm they do by digging up hedges, wild plants and the nests of the increasingly rare bumblebees. Each generation of badgers extend the sett they live in, excavating tunnels which can undermine open fields and even roads.

Many badgers are killed by traffic and in some places underpasses have been built beneath roads for them to cross in safety. They are also blamed for spreading bovine tuberculosis for which cattle are regularly tested and, if positive, slaughtered. Debate continues as to whether TB is passed from badger to cattle or whether possibly, as one theory suggests, a vitamin E and selenium mineral deficiency in the diet may be lowering the resistance of both badgers and cattle to the disease.

'Brock' is a fascinating creature but, like so many of our mainly nocturnal mammals, goes about his business unseen. In a few places farmers have built special badger-viewing hides for which they make a small charge. Patience is needed but as dusk falls the family of badgers will usually emerge and snuffle around looking for peanuts or dog biscuits that have been put out for them and of which they are extremely fond.

Above: A young badger cub emerges from its sett.

Below: Is TB passed between badgers and cattle?

171

Seed and Fruit-Eating Birds

As summer fades into autumn, insects become scarce but it is a time of plenty for some species of birds, as plants provide a bonanza of seeds, and fruits are plentiful on bushes and trees.

October is a change-over month, for the insect-eating summer visitors have already left and winter migrants begin to arrive. Some birds, resident in England all year round, are joined by arrivals of the same species from Scandinavia and the Continent if food is scarce or the weather severe overseas. They come, sometimes in great numbers, to seek the comforts of our more temperate island.

In some years the population of one of our most handsome birds, the jay (*Garrulus glandarius*), a member of the crow family, is dramatically increased with migrants from the Continent. Inhabiting deciduous woodland, jays are normally very shy but when disturbed they betray their presence with a harsh warning screech. A glimpse of white rump and electric blue outer wing feathers makes them

Above left: Jays have a passion for acorns in the autumn.

Above right: Goldfinches seek out thistles and teasels from which they extract seeds.

172

easily identifiable. In Spring and summer they are carnivorous and take eggs and fledglings from the nests of other birds.

However, in autumn and winter they become very dependant on acorns and in a year of shortage they will be attracted in large numbers to any oak trees bearing fruit. Sometimes jays are called 'acorn planters' because they store acorns by burying them in the ground, later using landmarks to locate them again. Inevitably not all of them are found and as a result, jays have been instrumental in helping to create woodlands.

Other birds also help to establish new trees and shrubs. Yew berries are much sought-after and distributed at random by birds. The flesh is harmless but the pip inside is poisonous and passes through the gut and is excreted. Hawthorn berries are another favourite particularly of blackbirds and the newly arrived field-fares (*Turdus pilaris*) and redwings, which are both members of the thrush family. These descend on bushes in small flocks to feed upon the haws.

Fallen apples in orchards or from hedgerow crab apples also offer a feast to hungry migrants as well as the residents.

Smaller birds can be highly selective: for example teasels are much sought-after by goldfinches (*Carduelis carduelis*). Some years, when natural food is scarce in Scandinavia, waxwings may suddenly appear eating the fruit of rowan trees although they are just as likely to surprise us by feeding on the berries of shrubs planted in super-market car parks.

Below: Each October, migratory fieldfares, members of the thrush family, arrive in England from their Northern European breeding grounds.

A Month of Mushrooms

Although some species of fungi can be found all year round, damp autumn days encourage the growth of the majority of mushrooms. Fungi either live as parasites or act as nature's composters by feeding on decay. The visible part is the fruit, but out of sight, mushrooms are equipped with a network of filaments.

About 10,000 different species of fungi can be found in Great Britain appearing in various colours, shapes and sizes although many can only be accurately identified with the aid of a microscope. Some are edible, others are inedible and some are dangerous: either hallucinogenic or highly toxic, although they may look similar to harmless mushrooms. Unless fungi are easily identifiable, expert advice is given or a very reliable reference book is at hand, it really is safer to say: if in doubt, leave them alone.

Many fungi and toadstools have a specific host or are most likely to be found in certain locations, so over the years some have been given very appropriate names. The most familiar, the field mushroom, is primarily found on open meadows grazed and compacted by livestock. It is unpredictable and great numbers sometimes appear in late summer when rain follows a dry spell. The horse mushroom which is similar, can grow large enough for just one to fill a frying pan. Parasol mushrooms (*Lepiota procera*) are also big and can be more than twelve inches (30cms) across. Giant white puffballs are another edible species, groups of which may suddenly appear in grass fields. Each one can be up to 2ft (60cms) in diameter and they are best eaten when young and spongy inside. They shrivel as they ripen and the spores turn to a brown dust which floats out if the puff

Top: A black substance oozes from shaggy inkcaps, otherwise known as 'Lawyer's Wigs'.

Centre: The distinctive Fly Agaric: one of many poisonous toadstools to be found in the English countryside.

Bottom: The parasol, like the shaggy inkcap, is edible and can grow to 12in (30cm) in diameter.

174

ball is put under pressure. Shaggy ink-caps (*Coprinus comatus*) also emerge in fields.

Within woodland the cep or boletus, also known as the penny bun fungus can be found and is delicious. Ceps are brown on top with a firm sponge-like underside, can grow up to 10ins (25cms) in diameter and are eaten by wild animals.

Bracket fungi grow on tree trunks. The most common is known as razor strop and is found on birch. Another, the beefsteak, is most often found on oaks and looks like a tongue growing from the trunk and inside resembles meat, exuding a red juice. The spores of fairy-ring champignon cause dainty fairy rings to appear on commons and heathland and 'honey fungus' (*Armillaria mellea*) is a common and very damaging parasite that lives on trees. Cup-shaped orange peel fungi grow on bare ground in woodland especially where the soil has been disturbed and bright yellow witches butter can be found on dead wood.

The stinkhorn, easily recognised by its phallic appearance,

Honey fungus growing at the base of a beech tree, a beautiful sight but an ominous sign for the tree.

attracts flies and is more likely to be located by its foul smell after which it is very well named. Several poisonous toadstools lurk within the countryside especially in woodland. Probably the best-known is the hallucinogenic fly agaric (*Amanita muscaria*) with its red or orange cap covered with white spots, always growing in the proximity of birch trees.

England's two deadly species are the aptly named destroying angel and the notorious death cap, which very few people survive eating.

Some fungi are tiny, such as the black candle snuff or stags-horn whose forked shoots can very often be found on dead wood. The mottled appearance of microscopic orange or coral spot can be found everywhere, covering dead twigs. Even more minute are the yeasts, moulds and mildews.

Ancient Woodland

After the last Ice Age, England was covered with natural woodland but around 5,000BC Neolithic man arrived on the scene and started to clear the trees, a process that has continued to the present day. It is estimated that one third of our surviving ancient woodland was lost in the 30 years following World War II, but that is now being redressed and recently, hundreds of acres of deciduous trees have been planted. However, it will be many decades before they begin to recreate the habitats that were lost.

Remnants of our ancient woodlands are now being carefully preserved in places such as Nottinghamshire's Sherwood Forest, (famous for its oaks and the legend of Robin Hood), Epping Forest in Essex, Savernake Forest in Wiltshire and the New Forest in Hampshire. Many old forests were not densely wooded and were originally established as royal hunting grounds by William the Conqueror as places where deer could be hunted and from which everyone else was excluded. Eventually, Commoner's rights were granted in the New Forest which today consists of a diverse mix of heath, bogs, mires and woodland. Verderer's rights permitted horses, sheep and cattle to be grazed. During the 'pannage' season, pigs could also be turned out on the forest to eat acorns and 'estovers' gave local people the right to collect firewood. Some residents are still able to exercise these rights when they are attached to residential properties.

Every species of tree growing in the forests had a specific use.

Above: Tawny owls are common residents in old woodland.

Often they were regularly pollarded (the branches trimmed off) at a height of six feet (two metres) so that the new growth was above the reach of large grazing animals. Ash is probably the most versatile wood, used to make spokes for cart wheels, handles for spades, axes and hammers and more recently Mosquito planes which fought in the Second World War. It also makes excellent firewood. Yew is the longest living tree with many English specimens more than a thousand years old. Yew and beech thrive on chalk soils.

The mighty oak, however, prefers neutral soils and can live for more than 500 years. Only two oak species are native to England: the common or English oak and the Sessile or Durmast oak. Although slow-growing, once an oak tree is mature, after about 100 years, it can support up to 1,000 species of wildlife from tiny insects through to jays, squirrels and deer which feed on the leaves and fallen acorns.

In a bumper year a single tree may produce as many as 50,000 acorns. The myriad insect and caterpillar species living on oak trees play a vital link in the food chain for many of our wild birds.

Perhaps the most important element in these ancient forests is the dead or dying trees and slowly rotting fallen timber. Holes in standing trees provide homes and nest sites for bats, owls, jackdaws, woodpeckers, nuthatches and tits. Dead wood harbours a rich supply of insects such as beetles, woodlice, centipedes, spiders and wasps as well as many species of fungi. The continued tidying up of dead trees has deprived many creatures of much-needed habitat and food and has had a knock-on effect on their populations.

Below: Dead or dying trees are important wildlife habitats in the New Forest.

The Wide Appeal of Fishing

Fishing is one of the most popular leisure activities for people of all ages. There are 55 species of freshwater fish in Britain and angling for them takes place not only on rivers and canals but also on still waters (ponds and lakes). Sitting quietly by the water's edge offers an opportunity to observe rarely-seen creatures such as kingfishers, watervoles or even an otter.

Species of fish are divided into two categories: coarse and game. Salmon, trout, grayling and char are classified as game fish. Game fish lay their eggs on shallow gravel beds known as 'redds'

and these are now being reinstated on some rivers. Rainbow trout are reared extensively to stock fisheries but for the real purist, 'fly' fishing on rivers for wild brown trout and salmon provides the ultimate pleasure. Hooks are disguised with slivers of hair or feathers to resemble the insects on which game fish feed and are floated on the water. The chalkstreams of southern England, in particular the river Test in Hampshire, are renowned for their trout fishing. Meanwhile salmon are returning to rivers across England, even the Thames. In the north, the Tyne which at one time was lifeless in its lower reaches, now claims to be the best salmon river in England.

Game fishing can be expensive so the majority of anglers have to settle for trying to catch coarse fish such as pike, perch, roach and

carp. Coloured spinners or lures on hooks are sometimes used or there is a wide range of baits available including bread, sweet corn and maggots. Coarse fish spawn in the Spring and are protected with a close season from March 15th to June 15th. Many coarse fishing societies restock their waters each year with fish that have been raised artificially in hatcheries.

Most rivers and lakes regularly fished are well taken care of with banks and excessive weed growth in the water kept trimmed. A rod licence issued by the Environment Agency is required by anglers 12 years old and over to fish and can be purchased from a Post Office or on-line.

Angling is an outdoor sport in which disabled people can participate. At a number of lakes across the country there are facilities for wheelchair users not only on the banks but also on the water in specially adapted boats.

Top: Dippers can often be seen on fast-flowing trout rivers.

Bottom: Seeing a kingfisher is a bonus for all anglers.

Willy Lott's cottage beside Flatford Mill in Suffolk, immortalised by the English Romantic artist John Constable in his famous painting *The Haywain*.

NOVEMBER

Sunsets are beautiful phenomena which occur only under certain weather conditions. The atmosphere is in a constant state of flux, comprising not of only gasses but also of billions of minute particles of dust and water. When the sun is low in the sky, its rays have to travel through a thicker layer of atmosphere than when it's overhead. Sometimes this results in spectacular sunsets but they cannot be predicted in advance. Some last for only a few fleeting minutes while others build up and fade more slowly. Sometimes, the sun sets like a huge ball of fire causing the sky all around to glow orange, like the Breckland scene above. Only as it disappears rapidly from sight does it become obvious how quickly our world is spinning. At other times when the sky is cloudy, rays from the setting sun are reflected in glorious shades of red, yellow and orange which only slowly ebb away.

181

Bonfire Night

November 5th is celebrated across the country with fireworks and bonfires; but no place in England can match the spectacular celebrations which take place in the East Sussex town of Lewes. Here, an earlier event is also remembered in addition to the actions of Guy Fawkes in 1605. 17 Protestant men and women became martyrs when they were burnt to death in Lewes during the fanatical campaign of Queen Mary I between 1555 and 1557, to re-establish the authority of the Pope. Early anti-papist demonstrations in Lewes were chaotic, with bonfires being lit anywhere and burning tar barrels rolled along the streets.

However, in Victorian times, bonfire societies were formed and things became more orderly, with each group managing their

Fireworks on 5th November: a celebration that marks Guy Fawkes' failed plot to blow up the Houses of Parliament in 1605.

own spectacular display. One of the oldest is the Cliffe Bonfire Society. Events of the past continue to be commemorated and the evening in Lewes commences with the laying of wreaths at the War Memorial. This is followed with torch-lit processions of people in costume, some carrying flaming crosses or dragging burning tar barrels, through the town. The night culminates with each of the six societies lighting its own bonfire and letting off fireworks on the surrounding hills.

In Devon, 5th November is celebrated in the village of Ottery St Mary with men carrying burning tar barrels on their shoulders through the town and in Hatherleigh where burning tar barrels are dragged through the streets on sledges.

In the centuries before flail hedge-cutters were invented, trimmings had to be raked up and burned. Many a farmer's family and friends have in the past gathered round huge piles of these to celebrate 5th November. The children made a 'guy' from old clothes stuffed with straw, and a pound or two was spared to buy a few jumping jacks, roman candles, catherine wheels and sparklers. Tame by today's standards, but nonetheless enjoyable at the time.

However, with Health and Safety issues and modern flail hedge-cutters which leave no cuttings to dispose of, many families now opt to attend organised events in local villages.

Few people today realise that bonfire night has pagan origins, which only later evolved into anti-catholic demonstrations. Most people are just there to enjoy the cheery winter spectacle.

Bird Watching in Norfolk

Birdwatching is a very popular year-round hobby. Some people are happy enough just to watch those in their gardens, others visit reserves managed by various bird conservation groups of which the RSPB (Royal Society for the Protection of Birds) with more than a million members and 200 reserves, is the largest and best-known. Knowledgeable bird watchers are able to identify a bird by its call or song which is very useful as small birds such as warblers are often difficult to see.

Catering for birdwatchers is a multi-million pound industry. Even people with only a passing interest will invest in a pair of binoculars. For the more serious a spotting scope which gives a clear much-magnified image is a must-have. A 'digiscope' enables a digital camera to be fixed to it so photographs can be taken to record the sighting.

Birdwatching can turn into an addiction and the 'twitcher' faction become obsessed with ticking rare birds off their extensive check-lists. A 'bird line' communication system exists to pass on latest information as to the whereabouts of something unusual. Fanatical twitchers will happily dash from one side of the country to the other and be satisfied with only a brief glimpse of it. Most 'rare' birds may actually be quite common in another country but only very occasionally appear in England, usually because they have been accidentally blown off-course from their normal migratory routes. Some which once attracted interest such as the egret are becoming more numerous, as warmer winters no longer deter them from staying. Others such as the avocet, harrier and bittern, are prospering as the result of conservation work. There are conservation organisations all round the country creating and preserving the ideal habitat for certain species.

Perhaps the rarest is the secretive bittern (*Botaurus stellaris*) which, through good management, is gradually returning to England's reed beds. This well-camouflaged heron-like bird is rarely seen but the deep booming call of males in Spring, the sound of which can be heard at a great distance, identifies their presence.

Above: 'Twitchers' and photographers gather on the north Norfolk coast.

Opposite: The bittern, one of England's rarest birds.

Bio-Fuels from Sugar Beet

Half of Britain's sugar requirement is home-produced from sugar beet, mostly grown on free-draining land in the east of England. Large factories owned by British Sugar process the roots to extract the 17% sugar they contain. The beet are washed, sliced and then brewed like tea. Evaporation of this liquid results in the formation of sugar crystals. Lime for use as a fertilizer and dried pulp for animal feed are by-products of the refining process.

The quota of sugar beet grown for food production has been reduced but the manufacture of bio-energy obtained from renewable sources is being developed. Liquid bio-fuels are considered to be carbon neutral because while they are growing, the sugar beet, rape and wheat from which they are manufactured absorb an equal amount of harmful gases from the air as is emitted when the product is used.

English-produced bio-fuels are also much more environmentally friendly than importing them from half way around the world, as has so far been the case. Sugar beet isn't sown until March, so the stubble fields in which they are due to be planted lie fallow all winter, providing food for animals and birds. Many birds such as skylark, lapwing and stone curlew find this late-grown crop provides ideal nesting sites.

Above: Sugar beet is harvested from late September to the end of January.

186

Bio-ethanol is produced from starch in plants and has 70% fewer harmful carbon emissions. In England this comes mostly from wheat and sugar beet. 5% bio-ethanol can be added to petrol without the need for any modifications. If higher, vehicles can be suitably adapted. Its inclusion is said to reduce emissions of carbon monoxide in older cars and will also help eke out our diminishing oil reserves.

Bio-butanol can be used at a higher concentration of up to 10% in normal petrol-driven cars. Bio-plastic can also be manufactured from sugar. In England, bio-diesel is produced from oilseed rape and sunflower seeds. Waste cooking oil can also be purified for use. It can be used in diesel fuel in much the way as bio-ethanol can be added to petrol.

Bio-diesel is naturally biodegradable and when spilt does not pollute either the soil or waterways. Bio-methane is produced by controlled fermentation of plant matter from which the gas can be collected and liquefied, in a process similar to that of the digestive system of a cow. Food waste and pig manure also produce methane which can be used as bio-gas.

It is said that all things eventually go full circle, for hay and oats were once grown to fuel the thousands of horses used for farm work! Following decades of growing crops solely for food, farmers are now encouraged to produce them for fuel. Recently Wissington beet factory in Norfolk has been extended to manufacture bio-ethanol from sugar beet. Next to the factory is a huge unit utilising the waste heat and carbon dioxide to grow tomatoes. Factories are also being built in Somerset and Yorkshire to manufacture bio-ethanol from wheat.

Below: Dawn breaks over Wissington sugar beet factory in Norfolk. Not as polluting to the surrounding countryside as it might appear: it belches steam as it produces not only sugar but also bio-ethanol and uses the waste-heat to grow tomatoes next door.

Regional Hedge Laying Styles

Before the invention of wire to confine livestock and mark boundaries, hedges were used for centuries in places where there was no stone to build walls. These hedges were mainly of hawthorn because it was easy to get established, fast growing and the thorns ensured it would be stock proof. The most effective way to maintain a hedge is to keep it regularly trimmed but gaps will appear if only the top growth is cut back.

Instead, every few years in autumn, a good hedge benefits from being laid. The old growth is partially cut through just above the rootstock, with a sufficient proportion of the stem left intact so it will continue to grow. Commonly known as 'pleachers' these are bent over at an angle and staked in place, creating a thick barrier at the bottom and from which new growth will sprout upright. A skilled man can lay 22 yards (a chain) of a hedge in a day.

Each autumn, hedge-laying competitions are held across the country, culminating in the national championship which usually attracts about a hundred entries. There are up to 20 regional hedge-laying styles suited to local agricultural needs such as whether they have to confine sheep, cattle or if arable is used in rotation. Also as a consequence of the number of hedges that have been planted along the top of motorway embankments, usually adjacent to post and rail fences, a new style of hedging has been added to the list.

Above: A veteran craftsman hedge laying in the countryside

The 'Midland' or 'Bullock' style is the most popular especially in that part of England where cattle are kept and corn is grown. The excess growth of the newly-laid hedge is only trimmed off the arable side while the livestock side is left bushy so that the new shoots are protected from the cattle by a barrier of old growth. Supporting stakes are driven in on the untrimmed side and a strong binding, sometimes willow, is used, woven along the top. In Derbyshire where there is mixed farming and sheep, the pleachers are firmly woven in place but there is no top binding. Northern counties of Lancashire, Yorkshire and Westmorland have similar styles with brush left on both sides and stakes staggered along the hedge but also with no binding.

In the south of England, which was once sheep country, the bottom pleacher is laid almost flat to the ground and the rest are laid at an angle. Brush is left on both sides making the hedge sheep-and lamb-proof and protected from browsing. It is bound on the top and known as the 'South of England' or 'Sussex' style.

Hedges that are laid on the top of high banks are known as 'flying hedges' and different styles of these can be found in Devon, Dorset and Somerset.

Above: There are more than 20 regional styles of laying hedges, but this Midland style is the most popular.

Below: The top of the hedge is tightly bound, holding the laid branches and the stakes firmly together.

Hedgehogs Prepare for Winter

Hedgehogs (*Erinaceus europaeus*) have been about for 15 million years. They were long-regarded as a carnivorous pest and had a bounty placed on their heads. However the Victorians found a use for them, keeping one in the cellar to eat cockroaches. Hedgehogs achieved a much higher status after Beatrix Potter created the character of Mrs Tiggywinkle. There are estimated to be about 750,000 in Britain although numbers are declining for several reasons. Many perish on the roads, habitat has been lost, dry summers make it difficult for them to find food and they themselves fall prey to badgers whose numbers are increasing. Hedgehogs are considered a gardener's friend because they eat slugs, snails, beetles and worms but out in the countryside they can be quite destructive in Spring when they prey on ground-nesting birds, their eggs and chicks.

Hedgehogs are unique in that they are Britain's only spiny animal. Each hedgehog has about 5,000 spines which are actually very stiff hollow hairs. When threatened, hedgehogs don't bite or run away but instead protect their head and soft underside by curling up into a ball. In this position they are extremely prickly and well protected from most things. They have a well-deserved reputation for being covered with fleas which thankfully can only survive on them. Hedgehogs are aptly named for they are very pig-like as they root about among the undergrowth, snuffling, squeaking and grunting. Their eyesight is poor but they possess excellent hearing

Hedgehogs are vulnerable in winter garden bonfires.

Hedgehogs need to build up good reserves of body fat in the autumn. In November they may seek out a pile of wood in which to hibernate.

and sense of smell. Solitary by nature they are very territorial, only coming together to mate. Fights frequently occur. They are surprisingly nimble and are able to climb, swim, run fast and travel up to two miles (three km) in a night. Hedgehogs are very accident prone and sometimes end up in places from which they can't escape such as garden ponds, tangled in wire netting or trapped in the pits beneath cattle grids.

They make a warm nest in which they hibernate between November and March although they occasionally emerge if there is a prolonged mild spell. While hibernating they lose a lot of their body weight. They are nocturnal and it's unusual for a hedgehog to be seen moving about during daylight hours unless it is sick. Increased activity at night occurs after heavy rain for that is when their invertebrate prey are also most busy. They have a rather strange ritual of producing lather in their mouths which they then lick over themselves. This is known as 'self-anointing'. Male hedgehogs are called boars, females are sows and their babies hoglets. After a gestation of about 30 days, four or five young are born in a leaf- or grass-lined nest. At first they are bald, blind and helpless but within a day or so white spines begin to show through, with brown ones appearing a few days afterwards. A sow may have two litters a year.

Many people like to attract hedgehogs to their gardens by putting out food but this has to be done with caution. Milk is not good for them: cat food is best, either dried or fresh each day. Fruit will also be taken by hedgehogs, with bananas said to be a special favourite. Hedgehogs need undergrowth to hide in during the day and a wood pile makes an excellent site for their winter hibernation, or special houses can be purchased. Winter bonfires are another favourite so these need to be checked before they are lit.

Wild Geese Herald the Winter

Whatever the weather, the arrival of skeins of wild geese around the coast and estuaries are a sure reminder that winter is on its way. Numbers of geese in England are generally increasing. Canadas and many Greylags are with us all year as permanent residents on many of our lakes and rivers, sometimes in pest proportions. In autumn they are joined by other species from the arctic regions in their tens of thousands. Brent geese, similar in appearance to Canadas but smaller, come to East Anglia and southern England from Spitzbergen and northern Russia. They favour coastal or estuarine mudflats and feed on the surrounding reclaimed marshes. Barnacle geese mostly prefer the coasts of Scotland and Ireland but can also be found around the Solway Firth.

Four species of grey geese also migrate to Britain. The largest is the wild Greylag which tends to stay in Scotland. The rarest is the Bean goose from Scandinavia which is mostly a visitor to the southwest. The White-fronted goose (*Anser albifrons*), easily distinguished by some white on its face around the bill and dark bars on its underparts, flies in from Siberia and is most likely to be seen close to the Swale estuary in Kent or the Severn estuary in Gloucester. Most common of all is the Pink-footed goose (*Anser brachyrhynchus*). More than one third of the world's population migrate to Britain for the winter from their breeding grounds in Iceland and Greenland. Some can be found on the Lancashire and Cumbrian coast but most prefer Scotland and the east coast of England down to the Wash and round the Norfolk coast. North Norfolk was always a favourite area for Pinks but many of the marshes where they fed were ploughed up during the Second World War and noise from air defences scared them away. It wasn't until 1976 that they began to return and now it is estimated that more than 100,000 Pinks regularly over-winter in Norfolk.

Pink-foot geese do not breed until they are three years old. They arrive in family groups and the young stay with their parents throughout the winter, migrating back north in February.

When they first arrive they feed on stubbles that have been left but when these are ploughed up and replanted, they seek out another source of food. With the marshes gone, winter corn would appear to be an obvious alternative but fortunately Pinks have a sweet tooth and are willing to fly a few miles inland to feed. To prevent these huge masses causing serious damage to their crops, some farmers

A mass of pink-foot geese feed on sugar beet tops left in the field by a Norfolk farmer.

delay ploughing after sugar beet has been harvested leaving the tops lying in fields especially for the geese. There they can find food enough during the day and at sunset they flight in their thousands to the saltmarshes, sandbanks and mud flats around the coast where they spend the night. It is an awesome sight, not only to see and hear them flighting to and fro at dawn and dusk, but also to see a muddy field heaving with a mass of dark grey bodies. Pinks are truly wild and naturally wary and there is safety in numbers, with thousands of eyes on the look out. They take little notice when a car stops but if someone gets out then it is a very different matter.

Above: Pink-foot geese arrive from Iceland or Greenland.

Right: White-fronted geese are winter visitors from Siberia.

Surprising Life in a Dead Month

November is a month when nature closes down and yet some things that have been inconspicuous for most of the year suddenly have their day. Evergreens stand arrogantly beside the stark skeletal branches of deciduous trees. It is now their turn to offer comfort to creatures through the desolate, winter months for they provide protection from wind, rain and snow.

Spiders and other insects too have a last fling before succumbing to winter's grip. Ivy is the latest of all plants to flower and bees which have been busy gathering nectar from other sources all through the

Spring and summer now concentrate their attentions on this one last chance to find food. On a sunny day in early November, ivy will literally be buzzing with bees attracted to its flowers. Hedgerow plants that are brown and dead are brought to notice once again when delicate spiders' webs woven round them are beaded with sparkling drops of dew.

November often seems a dreary month when nothing much is happening, but a closer inspection of plants reveals some not only still struggling to stay in flower but also, signs of activity on them. Having scrambled about among shrubs and trees unnoticed all summer, just when everything else seems to be succumbing to darkness and cold, old man's beard (*Clematis vitalba*) decides to put on a display. This

194

climber is England's only wild member of the clematis family and very much a feature of limestone and chalky land, particularly in the south. Its tendrils and tough mature vines weave through the twigs and branches like jungle creepers and in time become thick and very strong. Old man's beard can reach a length of 50 feet (15m) and live for more than 60 years. Gypsies used to smoke the dried stems. In the height of summer its clusters of tiny fragrant cream coloured flowers which later ripen into fruits are not very obvious. But as the last leaves of autumn fall, striking puffs of cotton wool are revealed draped over hedgerows and scrub almost as though they have been placed there as early Christmas decorations. These are the seed pods of old man's beard which are covered in long white hairy plumes, hence the very apt name.

Amidst the drab brown of winter hedges, when the sun shines through these feathery heads they look almost as though they have been lit up and it's easy to understand how the plant acquired its alternative name of 'traveller's joy'.

Opposite: Festoons of Old Man's Beard entangle an overgrown hedge.

Above: A honey bee feeds on ivy flowers in early November.

Right: Cobwebs drenched with dew.

Hedgerow conservation

That some of England's hedges are very old can be seen by the thickness of the trunks in the base of the hedge and the number of different species that have naturally become established within them.

Between 800 and 900AD, when the Danes threatened to invade England, Saxon Kings ordered that hedges be planted to protect villages. The first of several Enclosure Acts from 1750 onwards resulted in 200,000 miles of hedgerows being planted to encompass what was once common land. These were often planted in straight lines although sometimes there seems to have been no apparent plan. Some were probably grown to provide shelter and minimise soil erosion while others marked the edges of different soil types. In some places, long-neglected hedges either side of old tracks have run wild and formed belts of trees and scrub. In Sussex these are known as 'shaws' and in Hampshire as 'doubles'.

In the 1960s agricultural machines grew in size and needed more space to manoeuvre, so many hedges were ripped out to create larger fields. Food was a priority at that time and every acre taken up by hedges was seen as unproductive. As time passed, food production became less of a priority and then came the realisation of the extent to which our countryside was being destroyed. Grants were made available to restore many old hedgerows and plant new ones and gradually this past folly is being rectified. A mix of native species such as different thorns and field maple are already revitalising the landscape as they become established.

Hedgerows are the highways and byways for wildlife, often linking blocks of woodland together. They also provide food, shelter and nesting sites for animals, birds and insects both within the hedges and also along the bank on which they often stand. Few small mammals venture far into open fields, preferring the security and protective cover of hedgerows. A variety of plants also grow along hedge-banks where yellowhammers and grey partridges may choose to nest. Oak and ash trees have often been planted at intervals and many elm trees too once graced the hedgerows but sadly these

Hedgerows flanking a track in West Sussex.

have been lost to Dutch elm disease. These dead or dying trees now provide nest sites for kestrels and owls. A well-established mixed hedge bears many different fruits. In late summer, elderberries and blackberries are sought after by man, bird and beast. Hawthorn is usually covered with small crimson berries and the June flowers of dog rose will have turned into scarlet oval-shaped hips.

Spindle berries are encased in curiously shaped coral-pink capsules and sour crab apples look good enough to eat. Bitter bluish-black fruits cling to spiky twigs of blackthorn which birds mostly ignore but humans pick to make sloe gin. Country lore predicts that lots of berries bode a hard winter but it is actually the weather of the preceding Spring which determines quantity. Most years, established hedges are a riot of colour in autumn when fruits have ripened and the leaves turn to gold. Sometimes hips and haws will remain on the hedge all winter and conservation-minded farmers leave hedge cutting as late as possible or even cut just one side on alternate years.

Above: Rosehips provide wildlife with winter food.

Left: Hedgerow blackberries must be picked before 26th September – the old Holy Rood Day – for after that they are fouled by the Devil!

Far left: Bitter sloes steeped in gin make a welcome wintertime drink.

197

Free Range Hens

All domestic poultry are descended from the red jungle fowl of Asia. The majority of hens kept for laying are currently housed in cages which will be phased out by 2012. Meanwhile demand for free range eggs is constantly increasing. The cost is inevitably higher as providing these natural conditions is more labour-intensive and full of problems.

Free range hens (*below*) need to be fenced in for their own safety and shut inside houses every night to protect them from being massacred by foxes. To be classified as 'free range' there is a minimum space allowance per bird, both outside in the field and inside the shed. There are also strict regulations regarding hygiene and the use of medicines.

Large free range poultry farms keep several hundred birds in one unit. Hens do not need a cockerel to enable them to lay eggs, so only females are kept. All the eggs laid are collected every day, graded and checked. Under EU legislation if they are to be graded as class A, which most retailed eggs are, dirt on the shells can only be removed with dry sandpaper. If they need to be washed they can only be sold as class B or used for processing. Because free range chicken are kept outside, wet weather conditions sometimes make it difficult to keep the eggs clean as well-worn ground around the sheds tends to get muddy.

Another problem with free range poultry is that they are exposed to contact with wild birds, some of them migratory, which may possibly carry contagious diseases such as fowl pest and, of particular concern at the moment, avian flu. It is more difficult to treat them with water-based medication should they get sick because, as having access outside, they can often find an alternative source of water through dew on the grass, puddles or when it is raining.

In the knowledge that poultry can behave in a natural way, having the freedom to flap their wings, scratch in the grass, and dust-bathe, many customers consider that it's well worth paying a premium price for free range eggs or table birds.

DECEMBER

Christmas carol services are usually well attended in little village churches scattered across England. The round tower of St Mary's at Beachamwell in Norfolk (*above*) is indicative of early or pre-Norman times and several thousand-year-old churches can still be found. The few Saxon churches that survived the Norman Conquest were either relatively isolated or too small to be considered worthy of rebuilding. St Mary's is a fine example. It is a pretty little thatched-roofed church and the circular part of the tower with Saxon window-openings was constructed in the 10th century. Part of the north wall of the nave also dates from this time. The octagonal belfry was added in the 14th century. St Mary's is mentioned in the Domesday Book of 1086. Rectors of the parish have been traced back to 1278.

199

Mistletoe Auction at Tenbury Wells

There are more than 1,300 species of mistletoe across the world but only one (*Viscum album*) grows wild in England. Most now offered for sale at Christmas is imported from France. Mistletoe is a small, evergreen, semi-parasitic plant with sticky white berries in winter which are borne only by the female plant. They are said to be poisonous but are relished by birds, particularly the mistle thrush.

Mistletoe seeds germinate in crevices on tree branches, trapped in the bark when birds attempt to wipe the stickiness from their beaks. It prefers an open location, can grow on any species of tree but is most prolific on apple and poplar, especially in the south of England and West Midlands. For a century and a half, December markets have been held locally to sell both holly and mistletoe, most of which is gathered by farmers and travellers. Tenbury Wells in Worcestershire is famed for its mistletoe auction and it celebrates with an annual mistletoe festival during the first week of December. A mistletoe queen is chosen and celebrations include concerts, a ball

Above: Bunches of mistletoe growing in a tree in Shropshire.

Left: Mistletoe, thick with berries. In the 17th century it was customary to remove a berry with each kiss.

and a parade with Druids from the Mistletoe Foundation to bless the mistletoe.

Ancient Druids believed it possessed magical powers, was a symbol of peace and appreciated its medicinal properties. The custom of kissing beneath mistletoe dates back to an early Greek festival. In the 17th century it was tradition that a berry should be discarded after each kiss. The Victorians revived the mistletoe customs but, because of its pagan connections, banned it as a church decoration. In the Middle Ages it was hung from ceilings to ward off evil spirits and was valued as a cure for sterility, epilepsy and an antidote for poisons.

It wasn't until the 1920s that a renewed interest was taken in the medicinal properties of mistletoe. Rudolph Steiner researched its value as a treatment for cancer and in Europe a complimentary medicine called Iscador made from mistletoe berries is widely prescribed. Despite its toxicity, it is said to not only inhibit the formation of cancer cells but to stimulate the immune system as well. It is also sometimes used to treat irregular blood pressure and Hepatitis C.

Below: Mistletoe markets at Tenbury Wells, Worcestershire, are held every December.

December 'Spring Clean' on the Farm

December is a month for tidying up the farm. In all likelihood the ground will be too wet to cultivate, autumn cereals will already have been sown, and it is too early for Spring crops to be drilled. It seems incredible that the work now done by specialised machines was all done by hand until the middle of the last century.

Farm work was once a hard and very physical life; out in all weathers, having to manually handle sacks of corn weighing 2cwts (100kg) or more, milking cows by hand and perhaps walking all day behind a plough and horses.

Women too did their share of the lighter but often tedious chores in the fields as well as looking after a large family without the help of modern appliances. Very few men are now needed to work the land. They do so with more ease and in much greater comfort but each one of them needs to be skilled to handle efficiently the complicated hi-tech machinery.

Modern hedge-cutting is done with a tractor-mounted flail cutter which thrashes off the unwanted growth. If done regularly, the hedge is kept well shaped and tidy but if it has been left untouched for several years then the results appear to be an act of mutilation.

Not long ago it was teams of men wielding bill-hooks who kept the hedges trim. Conservation-minded farmers leave as much hedge cutting as they can until late winter so that wild birds can feed on the fruits of shrubs of which an old established hedge consists.

Teams of farm workers would also have been employed in winter digging out ditches to keep the land drained. Waterlogged ground makes it impossible to either cultivate the soil or grow crops. There is no need for ditches on light sandy ground but on heavy arable land, adequate drainage is essential.

It is even more important on reclaimed marshland, criss-crossed with dykes, for sedges and reeds stem the flow of water and if left uncontrolled would soon reclaim the land that was once theirs. In these wet areas, land drains have been buried beneath many of the fields. Once these drains were made from clay pipes but now, perforated plastic is used. Ditches are cleared by one man on a tractor equipped with a giant scoop on a hydraulic arm.

Above left: Flail hedgecutters smash the twigs to smithereens.
Above right: A ditch is quickly cleared with modern machinery.

DECEMBER

A fine cock pheasant in the snow. Pheasants were probably introduced to England by the Romans and are now a common sight in the countryside.

The Turkey and the Goose

White strains of turkeys and geese have been specifically bred for the table but all turkeys are descended from the wild black turkeys of North America. European explorers found that the Aztecs in Mexico had domesticated these birds and the first ones were imported to Europe by the Spanish in about 1520.

At that time anything which eventually arrived in England from the Mediterranean area was said to have come from Turkey which is apparently how the birds acquired their name. It is also said that six were brought to England in 1526 by William Strickland who bought them from American Indian traders.

Gradually turkey replaced the swan, pheasant, peacock and boar's head which had been popular in medieval times as part of the Christmas feast. Unlike chicken, which has become everyday fare, roast turkey is still mostly reserved for festive occasions and has become especially associated with Christmas. Fast-growing commercial turkeys have been developed with a disproportionately large amount of meat on the breast. Because of their conformation they are unable to fly or mate naturally and breeding birds have to be artificially inseminated.

The original breeds, which evolved over the centuries from their wild ancestors, are still being carefully preserved by specialist poultry farmers and have benefited from customers' renewed interest in purchasing traditional breeds. Probably one of the oldest is the 'Norfolk Black' which is very similar in appearance to the wild North American turkey, and as its name implies, was developed in Norfolk. A mature male turkey is an impressive sight when he displays. Like a peacock, the tail feathers are raised and fanned out, the wings droop and the fleshy red 'snood' hanging over his beak and the wattles beneath expand.

Geese have been domesticated for at least 4,000 years. The farmyard goose, once common in England, can trace its ancestry back to the semi-wild resident greylag geese often seen on ponds

and lakes. There are also many truly wild greylags that migrate to England each winter from the arctic. A few geese today are kept as watch-dogs, for they can be very vocal if something disturbs them. Roast goose is becoming increasingly popular at Christmas as an alternative to turkey.

Before modern transport, turkeys and geese were driven from East Anglia and other places to markets in London. Their feet were coated with tar and sand to prevent them becoming sore during the long journey, for roads were rough and stony in those days.

Above: Migratory greylag geese arrive in England each winter from Northern Europe. All breeds of domestic geese are descended from the wild greylag goose.

Right: The Norfolk Black is an old breed of turkey, noted for its superior flavour when kept in natural conditions.

Opposite: Free range white domestic geese.

The Rural Vet

In the grassland areas of England, farm livestock abounds and attending to it is an integral part of rural veterinary practices. Vets are called out to help with difficult calvings, sew up injuries and diagnose illnesses.

Farm vets have to do much of their work out of doors, often in difficult conditions that are far from sterile. Livestock are no respecters of conventional working hours and don't always choose to give birth, be taken ill or injure themselves when the weather is fine!

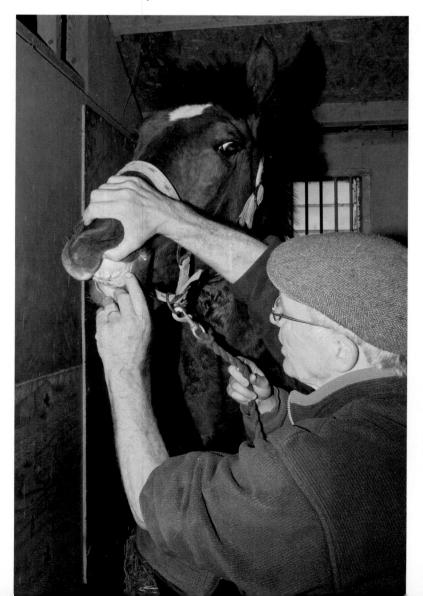

Much of a country vet's work is routine and includes the compulsory testing for diseases. A skin test is carried out to identify any possibility of tuberculosis infection, for example, and blood samples for cattle may be taken from a vein beneath the tail. Just as with humans, many infections, deficiencies and illnesses can be diagnosed through the blood.

To make working with large animals such as cattle easier and safer, they are driven one at a time into a small pen called a 'crush' where they can be restrained. Individual lifetime identification of all cattle is now a legal requirement and this is done by fixing a numbered tag in its ear soon after birth which can then be easily read and recorded. Each calf is also issued with a passport so that its movements off the farm can be traced at all times throughout its life.

Veterinary care of farm animals is costly and a call-out for a sheep can easily prove more expensive than the animal's worth but there are many preventative vaccines and treatments which can be used by the farmer. Experienced stockmen are fully capable of carrying out many of the necessary routine treatments themselves, such as worming or administering drugs prescribed by the vet. Inevitably though there are emergencies and the services of the country vet need to be called upon.

Left: A country vet checks the condition of a horse's teeth.
Below: A Cumbrian vet blood-testing young cattle.

Walking Whatever the Weather

Some of England's most popular walks bring out large crowds, even in the late December sunshine, so they have to be very carefully managed to minimise harm and disturbance to the environment. Paths have to be maintained to prevent erosion and car parks provided.

Beauty spots close to large towns and around the centres of favourite holiday areas, such as in the Lake District, Peak District and Yorkshire Dales, at times have to cope with a large amount of hiking pressure. For serious walkers it is still possible to get away from the masses by going farther afield on well-marked paths in the English uplands.

Alfred Wainwright was a very keen walker who mapped and published a series of eight guides to walking in the Cumbrian Fells. These have set a challenge for many hikers to reach the tops of all the 214 summits he listed. He was also the creator of the Coast-to-Coast long-distance path stretching 190 miles (305km) from St Bees in Cumbria to Robin Hood's Bay in North Yorkshire. There are 15 National trails in England, the longest of which is the coastal path around the south west peninsula. Stretching from Minehead in the north to Poole in the south, the trail extends 630 miles (1,000km). It is also possible to walk along the spine of England on the Pennine Way which stretches 268 miles (429km) from the Derbyshire Peak District to the Cheviot Hills in Scotland.

The new open access law has widened the choice for those who prefer to walk in solitude. Fortunately the majority of walkers are conscientious people who adhere to the country code by closing gates, controlling their dogs and leaving no litter behind them. Those who don't can cause much harm and suffering to both domestic livestock and wildlife.

Above: A couple return to Elterwater on a crisp December afternoon after walking on the Cumbrian Fells.

Roe Deer in December

Of the six species of deer to be found in England, only red and roe deer are native to Britain. Both have been present for thousands of years and Stone Age man learned to use the antlers of red deer as tools. During the 18th century roe deer became extinct in some areas of England and were reintroduced to these places during the following century.

Roe deer (*Capreolus capreolus*) do not form large herds but are normally found in extended family groups of up to ten. Although roe can be seen during the day they usually prefer to remain concealed in woodland and come out to feed at dusk. They are a medium-sized deer, standing 26-28 inches (65-70cm) at the shoulder. The coat is a rich red colour in summer and mousy brown in winter. Males (bucks) are territorial and the mating season (the rut) is in late July or August. Only bucks have antlers which they cast in November or early December and new ones covered in 'velvet' begin to grow

again immediately. Once fully developed, the horn hardens and the soft covering of skin dries and is rubbed off. The antlers of a yearling roebuck are only single spikes and it takes approximately four years before they become fully developed. Although mated during the summer, females (does) do not give birth until the following May. This lengthy pregnancy is due to the fact that the fertilised egg lies dormant and development does not begin until after Christmas.

A mature roe doe normally gives birth to twins which have spotted coats until they are about three months old. The young are left hidden during daytime and mortality is quite high due to foxes, uncontrolled dogs and through them being killed by farm activities especially during silage-making. Even so, the population of roe is expanding and spreading.

During the first half of the last century, when much tree planting was taking place, roe were regarded as vermin. This was because they were causing serious damage to young trees through browsing and bucks rubbing their antlers against bark to remove the velvet or to mark their territories. In 1963 roe were given legal protection, and since then numbers have been increasing and once again they are reaching pest proportions in some areas.

Wildlife warning reflectors, sometimes called 'wolf's eyes' have been placed beside a number of busy roads where there is a high deer population in an effort to reduce night-time accidents. These are angled so that the headlight beams from an oncoming car are reflected away from the road and across the verge, providing a visible warning for the deer.

Right: When alarmed the roe deer raises the hairs of the white patch on its rear, making it more visible. This acts as an alarm signal to the other deer.

Opposite: By early December, roe bucks will have shed or 'cast' their old antlers. These are quickly replaced with new ones covered in thick 'velvet'.

Small Birds Surviving the Cold

The same species of birds that feed in English gardens can also be found all over the countryside, proving that they are very capable of living independently of humans.

Many people put out a selection of food encouraging several different species to visit. Peanuts are popular with many of them, particularly Blue tits (*Parus caeruleus*), Great tits (*Parus major*) and woodpeckers. Some, like robins (*Erithacus rubecula*), will become tame enough to feed from the hand: one of their favourite foods is finely chopped cheese.

In ancient times the robin was regarded as sacred and still today, they have a special place in the English countryside for they are so easily recognised and there are few rural locations in England where a robin can't be found.

The Victorians invented the custom of sending Christmas cards and the robin soon became a seasonal icon. Postmen in those times wore red jackets and were often nick-named 'robins'. Robin sexes look identical. Most gardens have a resident robin which will follow close behind as soil is forked over exposing grubs and worms. While the robin may appear to be a cheerful, friendly bird, it is very territorial and aggressive and does not enjoy an amicable relationship with other robins. They are one of the few birds who sing all year and many a winter's day is brightened by the sound of a robin's song, although this too is part of their defensive behaviour.

They have appeared in literature for centuries, occasionally as bringers of good luck but there are also many tales of misfortune and sinister happenings associated with them. A robin entering the house was said to warn of a death in the family. Its breast was said to have become stained with the blood of the crucified Christ. Another legend has it that the breast feathers were scorched by flames when a robin took water to sinners waiting at the gates of Hell.

Robins can be heard singing all through the winter.

National affection for the wren (*Troglodytes troglodytes*) was recognised when one was chosen to appear on the farthing coins first minted in 1937. The Latin name of '*Troglodyte*' means 'cave dweller'. It was considered unlucky to kill a wren except on St Stephen's Day (Boxing Day) when it used to be tradition for boys to go on wren hunts. With blackened faces they would carry the tiny body of one around the village tied to a decorated pole, singing as they went, and collect gifts of money or food. Wrens are secretive and of all British birds, only their cousins the goldcrest and firecrest are smaller. However, for its size a wren possesses a remarkably loud voice. Males build several domed nests from moss, usually in crevices, and the female then selects which one she will lay her eggs in. Wrens rarely feed around bird tables but are busy little birds which search every nook and cranny on the ground and in walls for insects and spiders. In winter they will share a communal roost, often in an old bird's nest, which helps them keep their tiny bodies warm. Even so, many die in severe winters and the population is much reduced.

Above: Jenny is the affectionate name given to the wren.

Below: Blue tits and great tits are attracted to the garden by peanuts.

Hibernating and Fruiting

The winter solstice, just before Christmas, heralds the beginning of our true winter in England and some creatures avoid the unpleasant weather by hibernating. Although the winter solstice could logically be taken to mean the middle of winter, just as the summer one in June is misleadingly called 'midsummer's day', they both in fact seem to be only the beginning of the seasons.

Snails find sheltered places to spend the winter and wait for Spring. Often they hibernate in old walls or tucked behind plants but sometimes common snails (*Helix Aspersa*) can be found gathered together in their hundreds at the base of a tree. It will not be the lengthening hours of daylight that will make them stir but the rise in temperature. There are more than a hundred species of land snails in Britain but it was the Romans who were responsible for introducing the garden snail as a gourmet delicacy. Snails are prolific and can produce more than 400 offspring in a year.

Although land snails are hermaphrodites, they still need to mate with another snail to trigger fertilisation. After about a month, a large number of eggs are laid in an underground nest which, given the right conditions, will begin to hatch a fortnight later. Young snails do not reach maturity until they are two years old. Because common snails have moist skins, they are most active in damp weather and at night. They have voracious appetites and can cause serious damage in the garden and to agricultural crops during Spring and summer. In periods of very dry weather, they cease to be active, retreating inside their shells where they can survive for many weeks without water. Snails have four tentacles on their heads: two small ones are sensitive and used to feel; their eyes are on the top of the longer pair. Snails were once used to cure warts and cold sores and made into a broth to treat many illnesses including consumption.

Common snails sometimes hibernate in a great mass.

Just as the robin is synonymous with Christmas, so too is holly (*Ilex Aquifolium*). With its glossy, prickly green leaves and bright red berries, it is used as a Christmas decoration. Holly is widely distributed across England but doesn't usually get very big although a few specimens have been known to grow as high as 15m (50ft). Often farmers leave holly to grow in a hedgerow when all the other species are cut back. Tiny white flowers appear in summer but only female trees bear the familiar red berries which ripen in September and are much sought-after by hungry birds throughout the winter.

Evergreens were regarded as sacred because, unlike other trees, they bear fruit in winter and do not shed their leaves, representing eternal life. In pre-Christian times, pagans celebrated with a three-day Yule festival of fire and light shortly after the winter solstice. They believed that the return of the sun was encouraged by evergreen plants.

So began the tradition of decorating our homes with holly, ivy and mistletoe at Christmas, although it was considered unlucky to bring holly indoors before Christmas Eve. A massive Yule log decorated with evergreens would be dragged to the house by horses or oxen. Like the Yule candle, this log would be lit on Christmas Eve and it was believed that misfortune would befall the house if both were not kept burning until Twelfth night (6th January).

Afterwards the ashes would be spread on the fields to improve soil fertility. The word Yule is thought to have been derived from either the old English word Geol or Norse word Jol, both of which refer to the pre-Christian winter solstice festival.

The Christmas tree, however, is a relatively new idea, first adopted from the old German tradition by Queen Victoria and Prince Albert in 1841. The Feast of St Stephen on 26th December was the customary time to open alms-boxes kept in churches and distribute the contents among the poor of the parish; hence the day was called Boxing Day.

Holly is very often taken indoors to decorate our homes at Christmas, a pagan symbol of everlasting life.

Wetlands Balance the Effects of Global Warming

Development and draining have done away with many natural marshes and water meadows although there are now new incentives in place to safeguard what remains and to create new ones. In the case of global warming they may also prove to be of vital importance in maintaining water levels through storage in dry periods and affording overflow capacity when it's very wet.

Flood plains have for centuries been a natural way of coping with heavy winter rainfall. They help to alleviate flooding but many have now been covered with housing developments. The preservation of wetlands is also of prime importance for the well-being of migratory wildfowl in winter and many specific sites are managed solely as conservation areas.

Most reserves rely on cattle grazing the meadows throughout the summer to keep the natural grasses short. Droppings from the cattle encourage the presence of invertebrates and enrich the soil. When the marshes become flooded in winter, they attract thousands of ducks and swans from the Arctic regions who fly south to escape the worst of the weather. Numbers begin to build in October and start to decline in February as the urge to return to their breeding grounds grows stronger.

With warmer winters becoming the norm during the last few years, English wetlands are no longer frozen over for weeks on end. This means the wintering wildfowl are in good condition when the time comes for them to return north.

Wigeon (*Anus penelope*) particularly benefit from wetland management for unlike other ducks, they forage on land and feed on the grass.

As the last of the migratory wildfowl depart they are replaced by much smaller, inconspicuous summer migrants who head north from Africa to breed in our more temperate climate.

Throughout the summer months these same wetlands provide an ideal habitat for some of these such as reed, sedge and grasshopper warblers, as well as waders who move inland from the coast to nest.

Marshes also support an abundance of different insects and amphibious creatures. These form a valuable source of food for the birds that choose a wetland environment to nest and rear their chicks at this time of the year.

Opposite: Flooded marshes at Welney in Norfolk in winter create an ideal habitat for migratory wildfowl.

Above: A wild female mallard will rely on wet areas for food.

Below: Each winter more than 300,000 wigeon migrate from the far north to coastal areas of Britain, but only a few remain to nest in the Spring.

DECEMBER

USEFUL INFORMATION

JANUARY

Wassailing
Ryton Organic Gardens, Coventry.
Tel: 02476 303517
www.aboutbritain.com/Ryton
www.morrisdancing.org

Farriers
The Farriers Registration Council
Tel: 01733 319911
www.farrier-reg.gov.uk

Swans and Ducks
Wildfowl & Wetlands Trust
Tel: 01453 891900
Tel: 01353 860711 (Welney Centre)
www.wwt.org.uk

Riding
Riding for the Disabled (RDA)
Tel: 0845 6581082
www.riding-for-disabled.org.uk
Pony Clubs (riding for children)
Tel: 02476 698313
www.pcuk.org

FEBRUARY

Cley-next-the-Sea
www.cley.org.uk

Lynn Mart
King's Lynn, Norfolk
Tel: 01553 616200
www.west-norfolk.gov.uk

Alpacas
British Alpaca Society
Tel: 08453312468
www.bas-uk.com

Blacksmiths
British Artists & Blacksmiths Assoc.
Tel: 01526 830303
www.baba.org.uk
Gressenhall Museum of Rural Life
Tel: 01362 860563
www.museums.norfolk.gov.uk

Owls
Tel: 0870 990 3889
www.hawkandowl.org
www.owls.org

Clay Pigeon Shooting
Tel: 01483 485400
www.cpsa.co.uk

MARCH

Exmoor
Exmoor National Park Authority
Tel: 01398 323665
www.exmoor-nationalpark.gov.uk

Farmers' Markets
National Association of Farmer's
Markets (FARMA)
Tel: 0845 4588420
www.farmersmarkets.net
www.bigbarn.co.uk

Thatchers
Tel: 01858 575782
www.thatch.org

Rare Breeds
Rare Breeds Survival Trust
Tel 02476 696551
www.rbst.org.uk
Cotswold Farm Park
Tel 01451 850307
www.cotswoldfarmpark.co.uk/
rare_breeds

Canals and Narrowboats
www.canaljunction.com
National Waterways Museum
Tel: 01452 318200
www.nwm.org.uk

Chillingham Cattle
Tel: 01668 215250
www.chillingham-wildcattle.org.uk

APRIL

Widecombe-in-the-Moor
Dartmoor National Park Authority
Tel: 01822 890414 or 0845 345975
www.dartmoor-npa.gov.uk

Wild Boar
Tel: 0845 6014523
www.defra.gov.uk/wildlife-countryside

Tel: (mobile) 07790 454228
www.britishwildboar.org.uk

Dry Stone Walling
Dry Stone Walling Association of
Great Britain
Tel: 01539 567953
www.dswa.org.uk

Wind turbines
British Wind Energy Association
Tel: 0207 689 1960
www.bwea.com

Chatsworth
Tel: 01246 565300
www.chatsworth.org.uk

Bamburgh Castle
Tel: 01668 214515
www.bamburghcastle.com
www.castleuk.net

MAY

Corfe Castle and Steam Railway
Tel: 01929 425800
www.corfe-castle.co.uk
www.swanagerailway.co.uk

Helston Flora Dance
Tel: 01326 565431
www.helston-online.co.uk
www.helstonhistory.co.uk

Bluebells and Coppicing
www.woodland-trust.org.uk

Forest Parks
www.forestry.gov.uk/england
www.goape.co.uk
www.7stanes.gov.uk/england-summer

Coppicing
British Charcoal
Bioregional Charcoal Company
Tel: 0208 404 2300
www.bioregional.com

JUNE

Yorkshire Wildlife Trust
Tel: 01904 659570
www.yorkshire-wildlife-trust.org.uk

Appleby Horse Fair
Appleby Tourist Information

Tel: 01768 351177
www.applebytown.org.uk
Gordon Boswell Romany Museum.
Tel: 01775 710599
www.boswell-romany-museum.com

Jersey Cows
www.jerseydairy.je

Bee keeping
British Beekeepers Association
Tel: 02476 696679
www.bbka.org.uk

Bumblebees
www.bumblebeeconservation
trust.co.uk

Lost Gardens of Heligan, Cornwall
Tel: 01726 845100
www.heligan.com

Allotments
National Society of Allotment and
Leisure Gardeners Ltd (NSALG)
Tel: 01536 266576
www.nsalg.org.uk

JULY

Steam Traction Engines
www.steam-up.co.uk
Weeting (Norfolk) Steam Fair
Tel: 01842 810317
www.weetingrally.co.uk
Great Dorset Steam Fair, Stourpaine
Tel: 01258 860361
www.gdsf.co.uk
Thursford Collection
Tel: 01328 878477
www.thursford.com
Hollycombe Collection
Tel: 01428 724900
www.hollycombe.com

Deer Farming
British Deer Farmers Association
Tel: 01629 827037
www.bdfa.co.uk

Sussex Trug Maker
The Truggery
Tel: 01323 832314
www.truggery.fsnet.co.uk
The Basketmaker's Association
www.basketassoc.org

Southdowns
Tel: 01243 558700
www.visitsouthdowns.com
Downland Ranger Service
Tel: 01323 737273 or 01323 415255

Cricketbat Willow
Tel 01245 361639
www.cricketbatwillow.com

AUGUST

Moorland
Moorland Association
Tel: 01524 846846
www.moorlandassociation.org

Well Dressing
www.derbyshireuk.net

Cheeses
Specialist Cheesemakers' Assoc.
Tel: 0207 253 2114
www.specialistcheesemakers.co.uk

Cheese Fair
Great British Cheese Festival, Cheltenham, Gloucestershire Tourist Info.
Tel: 01242 522878
www.thecheeseweb.com

Butterflies
Butterfly Conservation
www.butterfly-conservation.org

Agricultural/Country Shows
Tel: 02476 696969
www.royalshow.org.uk
www.gamefair.co.uk
Tel: 0207 235 0511
www.cla.org.uk

SEPTEMBER

Norfolk Broads
Tel: 01603 610734
www.broads-authority.gov.uk

Dedham Church
Tel: 01206 322136
www.dedham-parishchurch.org.uk
Tel: 08444 848020
www.constablecountry.co.uk

Micro-breweries
Campaign for Real Ale

Tel: 01727 867201
www.camra.org.uk
Iceni Brewery
Tel: 01842 878922
www.icenibrewery.co.uk
Hop Farm, Paddock Wood, Kent (Museum)
Tel: 0870 0274166
www.thehopfarm.co.uk

Game Conservancy Trust
Tel: 01425 652381
www.gct.org.uk

The Fens
Tel: 01775 764888
www.visitthefens.co.uk
Wildlife Trusts
Tel: 0870 036 7711
www.wildlifetrusts.org.uk
Wicken Fen
Tel: 01353 720274
www.wicken.org.uk
Flag Fen
Tel: 01733 313414
www.flagfen.com

Pubs
www.heritagepubs.org.uk

OCTOBER

Tarn Hows
www.lake-district.com

Hallowe'en
www.woodlands-junior.kent.sch.uk/customs/halloween

Apples
Brogdale Horticultural Trust, Faversham, Kent
Tel: 01795 535286
www.brogdale.org.uk
East of England Project
www.applesandorchards.org.uk

Horse Ploughing
Suffolk Horse Society
Tel: 01394 380643
www.suffolkhorsesociety.org.uk

Badgers
Tel: 01422 846846
www.badgerland.co.uk

Badger Trust
Tel: 020 7228 6444
www.badger.org.uk

New Forest National Park
Tel: 023 8028 2269
www.thenewforest.co.uk
Woodland Trust
www.woodland-trust.org.uk
Bat Conservation Trust
Tel: 0845 1300 228
www.bats.org.uk

Fishing
Environment Agency
Tel: 08708 506 506
www.environment-agency.gov.uk
Salmon and Trout Association
www.salmon-trout.org
English Disabled Flyfishers
www.disabled-flyfish.co.uk
Tel: 01798 342222
www.wheelyboats.org

NOVEMBER

Lewes Bonfire Night
Tel: 01794 884040
www.lewesbonfirecouncil.org.uk

British Sugar
Tel: 01733 563171
www.britishsugar.co.uk

Hedge Laying
National Hedgelaying Society
www.hedgelaying.org.uk

Bird Watching
Royal Society for the Protection of Birds (RSPB)
Tel: 01767 680551
www.rspb.org.uk
www.birdnews.co.uk

DECEMBER

Beachamwell Church
www.group4news.co.uk

Tenbury Wells
Tel: 01584 810136
www.tenburywells.info

Mistletoe
www.mistletoe.org.uk
Mistletoe auctions
www.teme-mistletoe.org.uk

Wetlands
Wildfowl & Wetlands Trust
Tel: 01453 891900
www.wwt.org.uk

Walking
www.ramblers.org.uk
www.walkingenglishman.com
www.walkingbritain.co.uk
National Trails in England
Tel: 01242 533288
www.nationaltrail.co.uk

GENERAL INFORMATION

www.england-in-particular.info
www.aboutbritain.com

Wildlife
www.wildlifetrusts.org
www.bbc.co.uk/nature/wildfacts

Wildlife for Children
Tel: 0870 036 7711
www.wildlifewatch.org.uk

Heritage and Wildlife
The National Trust
Tel: 0870 458 4000
www.nationaltrust.org.uk

English Heritage
Tel: 0870 3331181
www.english-heritage.org.uk